CW00550277

ARABIAN DAYS

Tony Cawston died on 20th December after a short illness. He had not long returned from a very successful visit to Abu Dhabi where he lectured on the make-up of the Trucial States. The theme of the symposium was 'Memoirs of the Emirates through oral narratives' which Tony followed to the letter. Both authors had an audience with His Highness The Crown Prince Sheikh Mohammed Bin Zayed al Nahyan to whom they presented a leather bound copy of this book. This was the highlight of the trip and Tony's friends and family feel it is hugely appropriate that he so recently returned to Arabia and its people.

ARABIAN DAYS

Some unusual soldiering in the Middle East

Antony Cawston
and
Michael Curtis

Foreword by Major General Ken Perkins, CB, MBE, DFC

Dedication

This book is dedicated to the memory of

His Highness

Sheikh Zayed bin Sultan al Nahyan

and to the

Officers, Warrant Officers,

Non Commissioned Officers

and Men

who served in the Trucial Oman Scouts

from its inception in 1951

as the Trucial Oman Levies

until it merged with the Union Defence Force

in December 1971

First published in 2010
Second Edition
Published March 2011
© Michael Curtis
ISBN 0-9549044-1-9

All rights reserved. No part of this publication may be reproduced, stored in a retrieval system, or transmitted, in any form or by any means, electronic, mechanical, photocopying, recording or otherwise, without the prior permission of the authors.

This book is set in 11^1/$_2$ on 13 point Monophoto Apollo
Designed by Robin L. Oliver
Printed by Cedar Colour Limited, Chandlers Ford, Hampshire

Contents

Acknowledgements   vii
Foreword   viii

Part One

Chapter 1   The Lure of the East – Britain and the Gulf   1

Chapter 2   The Last Days of the Raj – The Indian Army   5

Chapter 3   The Levant and the Gulf – Arabic in Lebanon   20

Chapter 4   The Trucial Oman Scouts – 1959–1961   34

Chapter 5   The Trucial Oman Scouts – Some lighter moments   52

Chapter 6   The British Embassy Amman – The Kuwait Liaison
                Team   65

Chapter 7   Defence Attache – Lebanon and Syria   74

Chapter 8   The Defence Industry – British Aerospace   79

Chapter 9   Looking Back   92

Appendix A   Rulers and Senior Sheikhs in the Trucial States and Oman
                in 1959–61   169

Appendix B   Officers who served in the Trucial Oman Scouts in
                1959–61   169

Part Two

Chapter 1   Introduction – How it all began. Postings to Aden and the
                Trucial Oman Scouts   97

Chapter 2   Arrival at Aden – CALSAP – the course and arrival at
                Sharjah   100

Chapter 3   Joining the Trucial Oman Scouts, indoctrination, the
                headquarters and move to Mirfa and first roundabout   105

Chapter 4   Back to Sharjah, some sort of comfort as resident
                squadron   112

Chapter 5   Life in Sharjah, the proximity of Dubai, currency changes,
                the removal of Sheikh Shakhbut, ruler of Abu Dhabi   121

Chapter 6   Second roundabout, A Squadron move to Fort Jahili at Al Ain   128

Chapter 7   The Buraimi Hunt Ball & Point to Point   139

Chapter 8   Our stay at the Oasis and mid-tour leave   143

Chapter 9   Third roundabout, the move to Masafi, now in command of A Squadron   149

Chapter 10   Fourth roundabout to Manama and nearing the end, the last trip to Sharjah and going home   162

Chapter 11   The Final Chapter   166

Appendix A   TOS Order of Battle 1966-67   170

Appendix B   Salem Said   171

Appendix C   Characters along the way   175

Appendix D   A look at what it was like 20 years later   180

Appendix E   The Formation of the Trucial Oman Scouts   183

Appendix F   The Foundation of the Emirates   184

Appendix G   The Defence Forces   184

Further Reading   185

Index   187

Maps

Page ix   The Trucial States. Topography and political boundaries
Page x   The Trucial States and Oman – whole area of operations

Photographs

Front cover – Antony Cawston
Frontispiece – Michael Curtis
All the photographs in Part 1 – Antony Cawston
All the photographs in Part 2 – Michael Curtis
Except those indicated in the Acknowledgements

Acknowledgements

The authors owe considerable thanks to the many people who have contributed to the book.

Firstly, we are extremely grateful to Piers Gorman and Ultra Electronics Dascam for their great generosity in agreeing to sponsor the book. The publication of this book would not have been possible without them.

Secondly, we are grateful to Major General Ken Perkins for the time he spent reviewing the book and for the splendid foreword he prepared for us. His recent sad death means that he will not be able to see the result of our labours in book form.

Thirdly, our thanks must go to Nick Cochrane-Dyet for his help with this project, to Graham Barnett for the background information he has given us from his Trucial Oman Scouts archives and to Robin Oliver, our print consultant, who has had the immense task of making our drafts into a book.

Fourthly, we are very grateful to the following who have allowed us to use photographs and other information: BP, for the use of the photograph of Sheikh Zayed, the Orders and Medals Research Society for the use of the Defence Forces family tree and the British Army Review for the use of a map of the Trucial States. Our thanks too go to Mrs Stewart Carter for the use of her husband's photograph, to Colonel Pat Ive for permission to use his photograph and David de Butts for the use of the photograph of his father, Colonel Freddie de Butts (all from Bishop Michael Mann's book: *The Trucial Oman Scouts – The Story of a Bedouin Force* and he readily agreed also!)

Finally, we want to thank our wives, Celia Cawston and Rachel Curtis, and families, particularly Lucinda Curtis, for their time and support in the preparation for the final draft of the book and their help in proof reading, pointing out the odd error, some typing and scanning photographs. We also want to mention a few who have helped us in some way and apologise if we have missed anyone out. Our grateful thanks to Tim Ash, Rory Cochrane-Dyet, Joe West, James Devereux and Hastings Neville.

Both Michael Curtis and Celia Cawston are extremely grateful to Sam Chalmers for sponsoring the second edition. Tony Cawston knew about this in Abu Dhabi. He was delighted.

Foreword

Major General Ken Perkins, CB, MBE, DFC

Britain has never been a militaristic nation yet, more than any other, it has exported its military traditions and trappings around the globe. The empire has gone but its military has left a trail from the Far East, through the Indian Sub-Continent, the Middle East, Africa and across the Atlantic to the Caribbean. Uniforms, badges of rank, foot drill, the forms of parade and even military music betray British origins.

This inheritance of British military trappings would surely by now have faded had it been simply an export resulting from Empire. It might well have been eased on its way by the influence which comes with the military involvement of America as the dominant world power but there is little sign of this happening. When I served with the Pakistan Army in the late 1950s I might just as well have been serving in my own regiment at home. Invited back as their guest almost half a century later I still felt equally at home. British traditions had become ingrained by something much deeper than the formal relationship between British officers and the indigenous military.

In the days of Empire, and even when it had run down, there were countless opportunities for British officers and sometimes non commissioned officers to serve in the armies of developing nations. They went not merely as instructors but also in positions of command which brought responsibilities far exceeding those normal to their age and rank. Those who took advantage of this were seeking something more adventurous than available in a peacetime British army. Prepared to take the rough with the smooth, they were usually those who would strike a natural rapport with the indigenous troops they had volunteered to serve among. It was this rapport, which seems to come more naturally to the British military than others (pacé the French), which established the global trail of British Military traditions. Tony Cawston and Mike Curtis were part of this adventurous band.

Finding himself in a mundane posting after an enjoyable tour in the Indian Army in the days of the British Raj, Tony escaped to Arabia where he spent the rest of his military career and virtually the remainder of his working life. Mike was dragged kicking and screaming to Arabia and made no secret of the fact but on arrival in the Trucial Oman Scouts he found them to his liking and him to theirs. So much so that subsequently Arabia filled a large part of his life.

Tony Cawston and Mike Curtis were typical of those British officers who served in the Trucial Oman Scouts. Out of the eye of the Military Secretary their military careers were liable to suffer but their Arab comrades who adopted their traditions were the beneficiaries. Arabian Days is a colourful account of the exploits of these two officers.

Ken Perkins

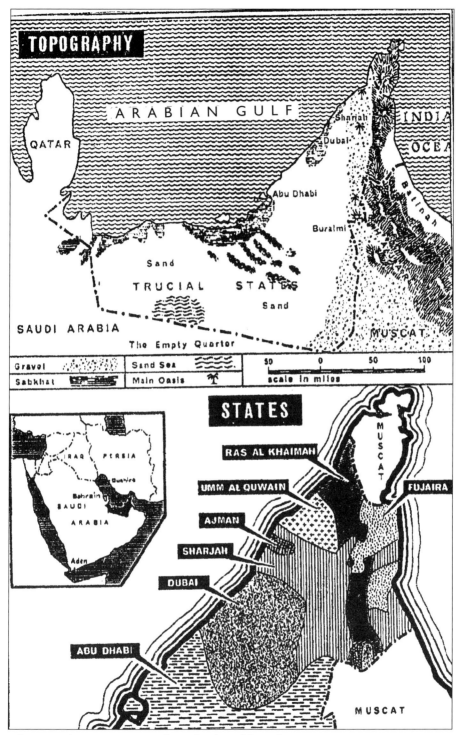

The Trucial States. Topography and political boundaries

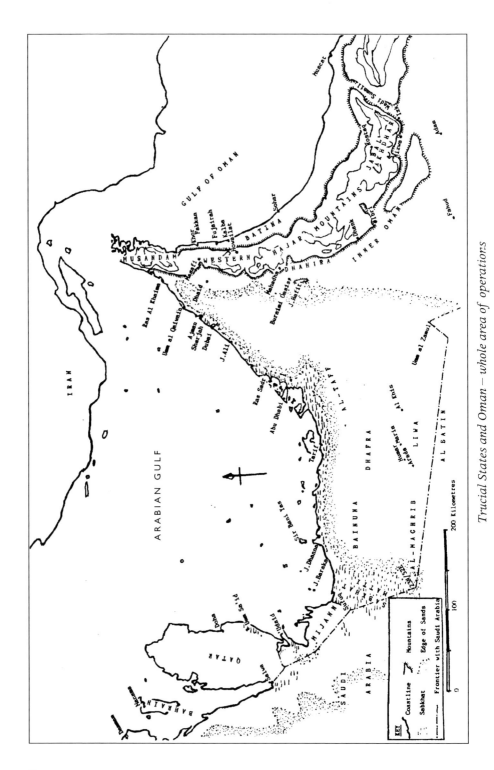

Trucial States and Oman – whole area of operations

x

Part One

A SCOUTS OFFICER
AROUND THE TIME
OF THE
JEBEL AKHDAR WAR
1959–1961

CHAPTER 1

The Lure of the East

This is the story of two army officers who each, albeit at different times, served for a period with the Trucial Oman Scouts. We each found such service far more interesting and fulfilling than normal peacetime soldiering at home or in Germany. We both now agree that it was a highlight of our careers, which significantly affected the rest of our time in the Army and also our subsequent lives. We both served and worked later for long periods in the Arab world where we met and became good friends.

The Trucial Oman Scouts was a comparatively short lived unit with a strange name and an interesting historical background which dates back to the heyday of the Empire and the British Raj in India. In those days, before the existence of the Suez canal, the Persian Gulf – or the Arabian Gulf as the countries of the Arabian peninsula prefer to call it – was a vital link between Britain and India and it was basically ruled from Bombay. The opening of the Suez Canal reduced its importance as a communications link, but the finding of oil, first in southern Persia and then in the rest of the Gulf, maintained its strategic importance to Britain, particularly to the newly oil-fired Royal Navy. Freedom of navigation in the Gulf thus remained a vital British interest which entailed a measure of control of the coastal kingdoms and sheikhdoms and their maritime activities. This was achieved by the permanent presence of East India Company warships until the middle of the 19th century, and later of Royal Navy frigates, but any exercise of control over these states stopped short of military operations on land except in an emergency.

An example of such an emergency occurred in 1809. At that time piracy in the southern Gulf was becoming an increasingly dangerous scourge to shipping in the area which the naval frigates found very difficult to counter. This was because of the very shallow nature of the coastal waters. Not only were they very shallow but there were many low lying islands and sandbanks intersected by shallow channels through which an armed dhow could escape from a pursuing frigate with ease, knowing that the frigate could not follow them.

Towards the end of the 18th century, frequent attacks on British and other shipping by dhows from the northern sheikhdoms on the southern coast of the Gulf were becoming an intolerable threat to shipping between the Gulf and India. The sheikhdom of Ras al Khaimah was the leading centre of this activity, described as piracy by the British, although recent Emirati historians have preferred to call it a valid dispute over the control of the trade routes. Some of its armed dhows were as big as a naval frigate and just as skilfully manned and commanded. British naval records attest to this. In 1809 a British merchant ship was attacked and badly damaged by a ship from Ras al Khaimah, the northernmost of the Oman coastal sheikhdoms. It was therefore decided that a military operation must be mounted to land at Ras al Khaimah and destroy the fort there in order to put a stop to such attacks. This operation was mounted by troops from Bombay and was a success in achieving its objective, but only for a time and, in 1819, it became necessary to mount another stronger operation. The town of Ras al Khaimah with its fort was sacked and its ships burnt in the harbour. Treaties were signed with the coastal sheikhdoms, then comprising Abu Dhabi, which had not been involved in the attacks, Dubai, Sharjah, Ajman, Umm al Qaiwain and Ras al Khaimah, to prevent any further conflict. From the mid-1830s, annual truces were signed by the sheikhdoms to prevent any attacks on each other's shipping. These were made permanent in the 1850s, giving rise to the name of Trucial Oman or the Trucial Coast. The name 'Oman' in those days was more of a geographical expression than a political one.

Another threat to British interests in the Gulf was the ever present possibility of encroachment into the area by the French, which was successfully prevented by the presence of the Royal Navy and the maintenance of close treaty relationships with all the coastal states. The importance of the Gulf as a communications link again became prominent in the 1930s, when Imperial Airways established an air route through the region with flying boats, using the lakes and creeks along the route from Europe to the East.

For many years the coasts of the Gulf continued to be controlled in this way, but no resources needed to be wasted in controlling the interior territories of any of the coastal states. This situation remained satisfactory for a long time until a new factor began to affect the area. This was the realisation that those interior territories might well contain reserves of oil, causing the consequent desire of the oil industry to gain secure access to those areas to look for it. Hitherto the area for centuries had no state or tribal boundaries. The tribal system and the devotion of the people to

Islam ensured a reasonable standard of governance. In the desert areas tribal disputes usually concerned water and the tribes jealously guarded their wells, but in the areas of sand and rock no one worried about lines on the ground, still less about lines on a map and the desert was free for anyone to roam in, just as is the case with the sea. And if the leaders of a tribe were dissatisfied with the ruling influence of a paramount sheikh to whom they nominally owed allegiance, it was not very difficult to transfer their allegiance elsewhere. It became plain that if oil prospectors were to do their job this situation would have to change. Both they and the tribes concerned would have to know exactly where the oil men could go and where they could not and, of course, if oil were discovered, this need would become paramount if meaningful contracts governing the extraction and marketing of the oil were to be concluded.

The first area in south eastern Arabia where this situation looked like developing into a problem was the area known as Buraimi. This is a small area of seven oases lying on the eastern corner of that part of Arabia known as the 'Empty Quarter' and is about a hundred miles south of Ras al Khaimah. Three of the oases, including Buraimi itself, are in the territory then known as the Sultanate of Muscat and Oman. The other four are recognised as belonging to Abu Dhabi, including what is now the city of Al Ain. In the 1950s, urged on by the Arabian American oil company, ARAMCO, a consortium of American firms, which was eager to extend the area of its concession, Saudi Arabia stepped up efforts to gain control of the oases in the Omani sector of the Buraimi Oasis.

The Empty Quarter is a desert wilderness so lacking in water that it is not even inhabited by bedouin tribes except along its fringes. Saudi Arabia claimed that Buraimi was on the eastern fringe of its territory and it set about endeavouring to substantiate this claim by sending tax collectors into the area, protected by a group of Saudi desert police. It also began a systematic campaign of subversion and bribery to persuade the Buraimi tribal leaders to acknowledge Saudi sovereignty publicly. The British oil companies with concessions from the Abu Dhabi authorities pressed for action to be taken against the Saudi efforts to extend their territory and the British government decided to raise a military unit, to be named 'The Trucial Oman Levies', initially using soldiers from the Aden Levies with British and Jordanian officers. This was the birth of the force later to be known as the Trucial Oman Scouts with locally enlisted soldiers and a body of British volunteer officers and NCOs. It was part of the British Army and subject to British military law and lasted until it was subsumed

3

into the UAE army some 20 years later. During that time some hundreds of British officers and NCOs served in the Scouts, most for the usual two year tour like the two authors of this book, but many for considerably longer.

Mike Curtis' experience in the Trucial Oman Scouts differs from mine in that he served in 'A' Squadron for two years, latterly in command of it, whereas I, a little earlier, spent two years as the chief of staff in the headquarters. We both look back on those times with great pleasure and value highly the effect they had on our subsequent careers. They led in each case to a fascination with Arabs and the Arab world and a preference for spending the rest of our working lives in the Middle East or dealing in it from the UK.

We have both made many friends in the Arab world, Muslim Arabs and Christian Arabs, and we admire their culture and their way of life which differ in many ways from ours. For instance I come from a family largely composed of people who worked in 'the City' and it was dinned into me that 'an Englishman's word is his bond' and that reneging on an agreement sealed with a handshake resulted in ostracism for life from the business community. I was sad to find, when I myself joined that community from the Army, that the prevailing attitude to an agreement that had become difficult to maintain had changed to 'Nothing in writing? Then forget it'. And I have found in my business career that I have several times had handshake agreements dishonoured, but always by a British acquaintance and never by an Arab.

CHAPTER 2

The Last Days of the Raj

Looking back on my army career, two periods stand out as being by far the most useful and the most enjoyable. One was my tour in the Trucial Oman Scouts and the other, which was in many ways a precursor which led on eventually to the TOS, was my time in the Indian Army. I found I enjoyed serving with Indian soldiers immensely and it was the Indian Army which led me into the less than conventional military career that was to follow. This came about because at the end of the war in Europe I volunteered, whilst still a cadet, to go to the School of Artillery in India to do a course there and to be commissioned. The S of A was at Deolali in the hills about 50 miles east of Bombay. Apart from the artillery school and ranges, Deolali was famed for its military lunatic asylum, whence comes the phrase 'he's gone doolali', but that had nothing to do with the gunners, although it did lead to ribald comments from time to time from members of other regiments. It was a most enjoyable course.

When that course was completed I and a very good friend of mine, Ian Greig, volunteered to go to the Indian Mountain Artillery. This was easy to do because all the Indian gunner regiments had been officered by the British since the mutiny a hundred years before and for an officer in the Royal Artillery, it was only a question of a simple posting once one had been accepted informally.

So Ian and I found ourselves doing a young officers' course at the Mountain Artillery Training Centre at Ambala in the Punjab. This consisted of training on the 3.7 inch Screw Gun, designed to be carried in pieces with each gun on the backs of eight mules, and on learning animal management, which included a good deal of time in the riding school. This was because the mountain artillery regiments were equipped almost entirely with horses and mules rather than vehicles. We also spent most of our evenings learning Urdu.

The screw gun was so called because the barrel was made in two halves joined by a semi-interrupted thread at its mid point. The two halves came together and a 90 degree turn of one part against the other locked them in place as one piece. This was necessary because the piece as a whole, barrel and breech block, was too heavy to go on the back of one mule and so was divided into two to go on the backs of two mules. The whole gun came to pieces and was loaded on to special saddles on eight mules. The ammunition went on two more. The actual drill was very much like the gun drill the Royal Navy do at tournaments, taking a gun to bits and slinging it across an imaginary ravine and putting it together again, but in the case of the mountain gun the mule saddles were an added complication.[1]

Learning Urdu was a high priority because an officer was not much use in an Indian unit until he had mastered at least the basics of the language spoken by the soldiers. One had to spend an hour or two every evening with a teacher known as a 'munshi'.

The Indian Army had a rank structure which was different from that of the British Army in that, between the usual British Army categories of 'Officer', holding the King's Commission, and 'Senior Non Commissioned Officer', the Warrant Officer, there was another category of 'Viceroy Commissioned Officer'. In a British mountain battery one had a battery commander, who was usually a major, about six captains and subalterns and then the battery sergeant major who was the senior NCO. That was the normal British rank structure, but in an Indian Army battery there were also three VCOs who were senior to the NCOs but junior to the officers. The officers were Indian or British and the VCOs were all Indian. The VCO ranks were Subedar and Jemadar and I particularly liked the modes of address between the ranks. VCOs addressed officers as 'Major Sahib', 'Captain Sahib' or just 'Sahib' and the officers addressed the VCOs as 'Subedar Sahib' and 'Jemadar Sahib'. It was a pleasing system of expressing mutual respect.

One of the duties that fell to me at Ambala was that of taking battery commander's 'orders' in the absence of the battery commander. At that

1. The essence of the gun drill was speed into action and gun detachment competitions were held throughout the Indian Mountain Artillery from time to time. The time measured was that between a fire order being given with the gun being in pieces on the backs of the eight mules in line ahead along a mountain track and an aimed round being fired from the gun on the ground. As the detachment was moving along in line ahead the order was given to deploy the gun and fire a ranging round on a given bearing and at a given range. The mules were immediately brought round into a circle by their drivers and the gun detachment assembled the gun on the ground in a series of coordinated lifts from the mule saddles; the layer laid the sights on the aiming point and set the range; the numbers two and four loaded the gun and the round was fired. I'm told that the record still stands at 57 seconds from the order 'Halt. Action front' to the report 'Shot'. On our young officers' course the best we managed was about three minutes.

stage my Urdu was still very weak, although I was trying hard to improve it in evening sessions with the 'munshi' (teacher). The battery subedar, Subedar Khuda Baksh, was a large and impressive figure, but his English was fairly weak and conversation between us was not easy. On one occasion various soldiers were marched up in front of me for minor decisions connected with discipline, other minor offences, granting of leave and so on, and a man appeared asking for a month's leave. I asked the subedar what he was entitled to and it appeared that a month was within his entitlement so I granted him that leave. A bit later another man was marched in asking for leave and the name announced was very similar to that of the first man, so I enquired if they were related and was told that they were indeed brothers. So I said "I've just given your brother a month's leave from next Wednesday, so I am granting you the same so that you can go off home together".

At this there were signs of disquiet in the room especially from the subedar, but I was getting a little impatient with his slightly irritating attitude, so told him to march the soldier out, which he duly did. When we were alone I said, "Whatever is the matter, subedar sahib, what were you trying to say? That man was entitled to a month's leave and there is no reason why he should not take it now." The subedar replied, "That's quite correct, sahib, but you have sent the two brothers off together". So I said, "What's wrong with that, subedar sahib?" At which he replied, "Well, the problem is that they only have one wife between them and so they prefer to go home separately". That was a quite new situation to me, but the problem could obviously be put right easily so I told him to sort the matter out to the brothers' satisfaction, which he duly did.

On another occasion my decision was again unsatisfactory but this time it could not be sorted out so easily. I was confronted with a blue eyed soldier from beyond Gilgit in the foothills of the Himalayas. He also was entitled to a month's leave which I granted him with immediate effect oblivious to signs of disquiet from the subedar. When the man had been marched out, obviously well pleased with the decision, I asked the subedar what was the matter this time. He replied, "That man, sahib, comes from a village many miles north of Gilgit and the passes will be blocked by snow long before the month is out and we will not see him here again until the snow melts in four months' time". The problem that time was that the decision could not fairly be changed against the man's will, so he had his four months' leave. I decided that I must enquire about these things more carefully in the future.

Our training at Ambala went on for over six months because there was a problem over where to post us. The end of the war in Burma meant that the mountain artillery regiments which had been serving there were being withdrawn to India and some were changing from the screw gun to other roles and other equipments. There was also the problem of the impending partition of British India into India and Pakistan which necessitated many changes in the army. Ian and I were posted from Ambala to a regiment camped in the Hyderabad jungle near Secunderabad. There was already a lot of preparation for partition taking place and this meant a fundamental reorganisation of the mountain artillery regiments which had always been organised with three batteries in each, one Punjabi Muslim, one Brahmin and one Sikh. Partition necessitated fundamental change and the newly formed regiment we were posted to consisted of three Punjabi Muslim batteries. Furthermore it had lost its mules and horses and was equipped with 75mm guns towed by jeeps, and it was designated to convert to an airborne role. We had some months in the Secunderabad camp near Hyderabad and then the regiment moved by train to Quetta in Baluchistan not far south of the northwest frontier and became part of 2nd Indian Airborne Division as 12th (Punjab) Parachute Field Regiment Royal Indian Artillery.

The train journey had its moments. Each battery had its own train and we officers did not much like the coach that was allocated to us and, since the journey to Quetta was to take about four days, we decided to camp on one of the flat-wagons on which the guns and vehicles were lashed. We took one of the flats and secured a Dodge 15cwt command post vehicle at each end facing outwards and camped between the two as if we were on a normal field exercise. There was plenty of space between the two vehicles for camp chairs and beds and a bit further away for a tin bath. We took turns to use the bath with our batmen producing hot water from the stations where we were frequently put briefly into a siding to let an express go through. Our train proceeded at a fairly leisurely pace through the jungles of central India with a station halt every two or three hours. I decided to have a bath on the second evening and had the water got ready but it occurred to me that I should make sure that I had plenty of time before we got to the next station. This was Jhansi, a big rail junction in central India, so while undressing I called to my friends who were having their evening whisky on a circle of camp chairs a few feet away and asked how long I had before we got to Jhansi. One of them who was keeping abreast of our progress looked at his watch and assured me that I had well over half an hour. I did not notice the sly looks which I'm sure were exchanged as I threw off the last of my clothes and sat down in the bath. I was enjoying the warm water and our progress through the jungle at a very moderate pace as darkness fell, when suddenly I realised that there was an unnatural glow up in front of the train and, to my consternation, it got brighter and brighter until I saw that we were entering a brightly lit station about the size of Waterloo station in London and as full of people on the platforms as Waterloo is at the height of the rush hour. I yelled for a towel to cover myself with and was only greeted with raucous laughter until one of my friends relented and threw me a bath towel. The train stopped in the station between the crowded platforms, mercifully not for very long, while I lay in the tin tub with the towel across my middle, trying to look as if this was a common occurrence for me on train journeys, until the train slowly started to move again and we went off into the night. I saw the joke at that stage and got dressed and someone poured me a double whisky, which came as a very welcome anticlimax as we returned to our steady progress through the now dark jungle.

Training continued in Quetta and we all went on parachute courses at Rawalpindi which consisted of 8 jumps from a Dakota. The part of that course I best remember was being on the ground on the DZ (dropping zone)

A stick of 5 jumping from a Dakota

after landing, gathering up my parachute, and suddenly being warned to look up to where a 'stick' of Gurkhas was emerging from a Dakota overhead. The point was that on leaving the aircraft one was supposed to unstrap the equipment bag from one's leg and lower it ten feet or so on its rope so that it would hit the ground a second or so before one's feet did. The Gurkhas tended to let the bag drop freely to the end of its rope thus causing it, as often as not, to break away and descend like a bomb on anyone standing on the DZ below. It was wise therefore, whenever Gurkhas were liable to be jumping, to keep a wary eye skywards if one was on the DZ.

Two things made Quetta thoroughly enjoyable for me. The first was the opportunity to take up deer stalking in the mountains surrounding the

My OP 'ack' (assistant), Boota Khan, during parachute training, 1947

My OP 'ack', Boota Khan, waiting for the green light

city. In fact there were no deer, but there were wild sheep and wild goats. The sheep were urial and the goats were markhor. The latter were large goats with long straight but spiral horns. They could walk along apparently sheer rock faces and had eyesight which equalled that of a well sighted human with x 8 binoculars. If you could see this animal through binoculars you could be certain that he could see you, especially if you moved, so stalking required a great deal of care and patience. Quetta itself lies in a long narrow valley at 5,000 feet above sea level. The surrounding mountains rise to 10,000 feet and are snow covered in winter. That is where the wild sheep and goats live, the sheep on the lower slopes. The other factor which makes stalking difficult is the silence in the mountains. In comparison deer stalking in Scotland is child's play because some sort of movement is nearly always noticeable in the distance as is some distant sound of traffic and deer are therefore accustomed to movement and sound. Stalking in Baluchistan required a long approach march of a day or so to get to the most likely mountains and then long days of rambling climbing to locate the quarry. It made a most wonderful long weekend.

The Quetta Hunt, 1946

'Shaitan' – the 20-year-old hunter

The other most enjoyable activity was hunting. The Quetta officers' club ran a pack of hounds which hunted twice a week and it was all included in one's club subscription. There also seemed to be horses always available and I was lent a wonderful horse by someone who was off to the UK on long leave. He lasted me for one whole season and was a great jumper. The Quetta valley is long and fertile with the mountains running along on either side. There were no foxes, or if there were they would have been in the hills or the desert. What we hunted were jackal and usually we found scent at one end of the valley and then had a ten mile gallop down the valley to the other end. The next time we probably did the same in reverse. The Master of Foxhounds in my time was a Major Birley from the British airborne light artillery regiment stationed there. He was a good MFH and wonderful on a hunting horn, but ran into trouble on his parachute course, damaging an ankle on the 7th jump. He came back to the regiment in Quetta and put up his wings on his uniform, only to be told sternly by his colonel to take them down because he had not completed the course of 8 jumps. That was rather bad luck for him but one can't wear 7/8ths of a pair of wings.

The CO of 12th Regiment was Lieutenant Colonel Kumaramangalam, a famous character in the Indian artillery who had been commissioned into the Royal Artillery (British), served in the Western Desert in the war and later rose to be chief of staff of the Indian Army. He was the son of the Prime Minister of Madras and was a product of Eton and Sandhurst. Being southern Indian he spoke very little Urdu which the Punjabis spoke and he also insisted on having only British officers posted in to the regiment and no Indians, so when the troops had to be gathered together and spoken to about anything one of the British officers had to be deputed to do the speaking. There was an amusing story told me by a friend in the British regiment stationed in Quetta. They invited Colonel K to dinner and in the mess after the meal gently chided him because on a recent live firing exercise our regiment had dropped a shell short, not far from the British regiment's gun position. He merely grinned and apologised saying, "Sorry about that, chaps, but it is a bit difficult training these wogs to shoot straight you know." It seemed all right coming from him because he was very dark skinned, but the term 'wog' was absolutely taboo in the Indian Army, especially amongst the British officers, none of whom would dream of using it.

I stayed with 12th Regiment until the British left India on partition in 1947. It was the leading Muslim politician Mohammed Ali Jinnah who

Lt Col Kumaramangalam, CO 12 (Punjab) Parachute Field Regiment, Royal Indian Artillery (later CGS Indian Army)

insisted on the formation of a purely Muslim state when the British left India. No one wanted this except the party Jinnah headed. Senior Indians and British in the government were fearful of the consequences of such a split, but the insistence of the new Labour government in the UK and of Viscount Mountbatten, the last Viceroy, that the British withdrawal should be accelerated as fast as possible, led to the idea being accepted. The worst fears of the doubters were realised in the subsequent religious massacres in the Punjab.

The Punjab, the land of the five rivers, was a state as big as England with a population of 80 million composed of roughly equal proportions of Hindus, Sikhs and Muslims, most living in villages each composed of one religion and scattered randomly across the length and breadth of the state. Unfortunately the planners who decided on the future borders of India and the new Muslim state, Pakistan, felt that they had to divide the Punjab in two. The new border ran through the area of Ambala where I had done my young officers' course in the mountain artillery. The approach of the date of partition meant that the Muslims in the east of the Punjab felt that they should move to the west and the Hindus and Sikhs living in the area allotted to Pakistan became anxious to move to the east. Despite the exhortations of the politicians on both sides that people should remain where they were, movement of people began and inevitably incidents of violence between the religious groups started. These rapidly escalated until the whole area was in a state of panic with thousands of people moving in each direction. Massacres occurred, particularly on the main east-west railway which ran through the Punjab. Trains full of Muslims going west were stopped by Hindus and all the passengers taken out and killed and vice versa. British passengers were powerless to intervene and were told that they were in no danger if they sat still, but that they would be killed if they tried to intervene. Many thousand Punjabis died in this way and in Quetta, where many of the Muslim trains ended, hundreds of Muslim passengers arrived dead or viciously mutilated. It was a horrifying period which could have been avoided if there had been no partition or if it had been conducted in a properly planned and deliberate fashion as the senior planners in the Indian government had wanted. The population of the new state of Pakistan was about 100 million after partition with very few people other than Muslims in it, but the Muslims remaining in post-partition India were twice that number. Partition was in fact never strictly necessary except to satisfy the ambitions of the small Muslim political classes in the west.

I was very nearly an unwitting party to a terrible crime in Quetta before the beginning of the massacres. I was mess secretary at the time and our Hindu mali, the mess gardener, came to me and said that he wanted to be paid off so that he could go east with his family. When I asked him why he wanted to go he prevaricated and finally said that he was afraid of what might happen in Quetta and that he was afraid of the Muslims. The Muslims were, of course, the overwhelming majority of the population locally, but at the time the massacres in the Punjab had not begun. I calmed

The mali (gardener) at the Quetta mountain artillery officers mess

him down and said I was sure he had nothing to worry about and that we valued him as our mali because he kept the mess garden so well. So he went away. The following month he came to me again with the same worries. This time my bearer was present, a very cheerful and competent man, a Muslim of course, and I turned to him and said I was sure that he and his friends would not dream of hurting the mali or his family. At that my

16

bearer, Yusuf, grinned broadly and assured the mali that he was perfectly safe. Another two weeks went by and again, on pay day, the mali in an agitated way asked yet again to be finally paid off. So reluctantly I did as he asked and said goodbye to him.

Thank God I did so, because barely a month later the news came to us that another Hindu mali, who worked as a mess gardener and who lived by the railway track near where our man had lived, had been found brutally murdered along with his wife and their two children. We were all horrified at this and no one more than I was. I remembered this for a very long time, thanking heaven that I had let our man go. I am certain that, had I not done

My bearer, Yusuf at Quetta

so, he and his family would have met the same fate and it would have been on my conscience for the rest of my life.

The latter part of my service in India was a depressing period. The regiment was gradually disbanded and my final task in the last few months was as regimental quartermaster. In the British Army this job is normally done by a senior warrant officer who has been commissioned into the post, but in the Indian Army the quartermaster was a regimental officer on a par with the adjutant. So in my case I went from being a battery captain, second in command of a battery, to the job of quartermaster, charged with getting rid of all the regiment's stores and equipment. This included one hundred jeeps, twenty four 75 mm guns and masses of other equipment. I was ably assisted by a VCO, a jemadar quartermaster, who managed to solve one or two difficult problems which I found very worrying. For instance one day on my twice weekly check on the one hundred jeeps which were by then all on my sole charge I found that two were missing. All that remained of them were their number plates, front and rear, which had been carefully left on the ground where the vehicles had been the night before. Frantic enquiries were quite fruitless and I summoned the jemadar quartermaster and asked him if he had any ideas on what to do about the situation. He said he would see what he could do and report back.

Fortunately we were not the only unit in Quetta which was disbanding and the jemadar sahib appeared the next morning and said that he had solved the problem. I asked him how he had achieved such a feat. "Well sahib," he said, "I did not tell you before, but we happen to have four hundred greatcoats which are not on charge and a quartermaster friend of mine the other side of the garrison is short of greatcoats and he has given me two jeeps in exchange for our greatcoats." In normal times this sort of thing would obviously have been quite impossible and there would have been courts of inquiry into the whole matter, but these times were far from normal and that was the end of the problem.

Another problem which I found amusing in the end occurred when the final accounting procedures were nearly complete. The civilian auditors had been through all my files and account books and then paid me a final visit. I was a little worried at the prospect of this visit because one problem I had been unable to solve was that ten prismatic compasses were missing. Obviously some of the officers had left the regiment without handing them in and in those days they cost ten pounds each, so I was faced with the possibility of having to pay a hundred pounds to make good the loss. This would have been quite a large sum out of my pay in those days. I had therefore decided to try a bit of sleight of hand in the relevant account book and made out a voucher transferring the ten 'compasses prismatic' to the page headed 'compasses dividable' and went down to the bazaar and bought ten school geometry compasses for the store in the hope that the auditors might not spot the subterfuge.

On the day of the auditors' final visit I gave them a good lunch and congratulated them on their work. "There's just one point I wish to ask you about," said the head auditor. "I notice that you have amalgamated two pages in the accounts into one which now covers two sorts of compasses. Are they the same thing?" "Well," I said, "They're all just compasses and fairly small items, so I thought it would simplify the accounts if I put them all on one page." "Oh that's all right then," said the head auditor, "I thought there would be a simple explanation. I think it's time we were off. Thanks so much for lunch." And with that they left!

So I left India, feeling sad that I had not served in the Indian Army earlier, but cheering myself with the thought that, had I done so, I might well have ended my life prematurely in the war in Burma. I decided that the sensible thing to do was to look out for a similar posting in the future.

CHAPTER 3

The Levant and the Gulf

I returned from India to the UK at the end of 1947 and served for a time with 33rd Airborne Light Regiment RA. I then went up to Cambridge in order to get a law degree in case I later decided to leave the Army, after which I found myself posted to a heavy anti-aircraft regiment in Cheshire. When I protested that I had no interest at all in Heavy AA I was told that all gunner officers had to do time in AA units because such units by then comprised about half of the strength of the Royal Artillery. But everyone was beginning to realise that the new generation of bombers flew too fast for the mechanical computers then in service in AA units to follow them across the sky and also too high for the 3.7 inch AA guns then in service to be able to reach them. So it was a depressing time to be serving in AA Command and I determined to get out of it as soon as I could. This was not easy to do without resigning one's commission and that I did not want to do. I decided to apply to go to the Arab Legion in Jordan which was largely officered by British officers and was commanded by General Glubb. My idea was that service with Arab troops would probably be as enjoyable as I had found service with Indian troops to be. Furthermore they would all be volunteers, whereas the British Army at that time consisted largely of conscripts whose main aim was to do their time and get 'demobbed' as soon as possible. Unfortunately AA Command would not let me go and I had to serve on in Cheshire. This was disappointing but there were compensations. The regiment was near Knutsford and it was a very pleasant part of England. My then wife, Mary, and I had a delightful Elizabethan cottage where our daughter, Caroline, was born in 1952. Life was enjoyable but I still hankered to get overseas. And then I came across an order in Army Council Instructions which said that officers were encouraged to volunteer to learn Arabic at the Middle East Centre for Arab Studies in Lebanon. The important thing was that the Instruction stated that 'applications will not be withheld for any reason'. So, thinking that this was a good way to get to the Arab Legion in due course, I applied and was accepted.

This decision was one that decisively affected my career, both for the rest of my time in the Army and later after I retired from the service. The course lasted about nine months and I ended up with a thorough knowledge of the Middle East and the top grade of interpretership. But, by the time the course at MECAS ended, part of my original reason for doing it was nullified by the fact that King Hussein, under pressure from the rest of the Arab world, had sacked Glubb from the command of the Arab Legion in Jordan and nearly all the remaining British officers had left.

However, I did have a short time with the Arab Legion while I was at MECAS. From time to time during the course there were breaks when we were encouraged to go off somewhere to practise some colloquial Arabic. On such an occasion I went off to Jordan to spend two weeks in one of the Jordan Arab Legion's desert patrol frontier forts where none of the residents spoke any English at all. There was a sergeant and about a dozen soldiers and about a dozen camels. Their duty was to patrol the Jordan frontier along to the next post and back every two weeks or so. Each post was a four square mud brick fort and there must have been about twenty of these along the northern, eastern and southern frontiers of the country.

My people in the fort I was allocated to at Station H4 on the pipeline from Iraq to the Mediterranean coast were very friendly and we got on well, although I was surprised to find how much the soldiers' sex lives dominated their conversation. I don't know why I was surprised, but I had somehow thought that the noble bedouin of the desert thought more about higher things. However I learnt a lot of new words that could well be of use in military service in the area, but were no good to me at all in my later diplomatic postings.

I had one exciting incident during my stay. One of the soldiers told me that they had been invited to a wedding in a nearby village and asked me if I would like to come too. This seemed a good thing to do, so the next day I found myself being taught how to mount a couched camel for a ride across the desert to the village whose palm tree tops were just visible behind a sand dune on the horizon. The motion when the camel rose to its feet nearly unseated me but after that I felt fairly comfortable, although I sorely missed a proper saddle and proper reins. In fact I was sitting on a rudimentary saddle and in my hands only held a rope attached somehow to the animal's mouth, but with no bit. However, we set off, I in front, followed by three of my new friends on their camels behind me. They said, "That's fine, just head for those palm trees in the distance. You can't go wrong". So we proceeded tranquilly across the desert. After a time I heard some giggling behind me which was quickly suppressed but when I glanced round at another snigger, I was just in time to see one of my companions with his camel stick stretched out at the end of his arm delivering a rapier like lunge with it up the tenderest part of my animal's backside. This resulted in a peculiar strangled cry from the camel and an immediate surge into a mad gallop. I was horrified to see when I looked down at the ground that it seemed far away but going past at a frightening speed with the animal's legs appearing to be all over the place and quite uncontrolled. I frantically pulled on the rope which was the only substitute for reins but, there being no bit, the only result was that the animal's head was pulled round at the end of its long neck until it faced me crouched on its back. There was this great head facing backwards towards me with its lips dribbling froth while it continued to gallop forwards with its legs seemingly floundering about in all directions. I knew how to control a runaway horse but I was completely defeated by this runaway camel. All I could do was to hang on to its rump while it continued its mad gallop, ending up in the middle of the village where the wedding was. There it stopped in the village square and sank exhausted to its knees enabling me to slide off on to the ground with a sigh of relief. Everyone thought the whole thing uproariously funny and once my feet were again on the ground I had to acknowledge that it must have seemed very funny to the onlookers. On the way back to the fort I was allowed a comfortable ride.

At the end of the course at MECAS it was suggested that I should volunteer for the Trucial Oman Levies as they still were called at that time. I now sometimes wish that I had gone to the Levies then but conventional military thinking prevailed and I decided I must get on with working for the Staff College exam. So I opted for a staff job in the Canal Zone. This was based on the assumption that Buraimi, where the TOL were deployed, was not the ideal place to work for an exam based on the essentially traditional structure of the British army. There followed service in Libya and then the Staff College, after which I found myself in 32 Medium Regiment in Carlisle.

I was posted from Carlisle to Bahrain in midsummer 1958. Iraq was threatening to annex Kuwait for whose security and defence we, the British, were still responsible and so it was decided to reinforce the British military presence in the Gulf. On the army side a second battalion was sent to Bahrain and a brigade was placed on alert in Aden. The HQ in Bahrein acquired an additional half a dozen extra staff officers of whom I was one. The HQ was called Land Forces Persian Gulf (LFPG).

In the event the Iraqi threat receded and the extra staff officers in HQLFPG found themselves with little to do, but a different military problem was festering away at the other end of the Gulf, where we also had defence responsibilities. This was the rebellion against the Sultan of Oman by the tribes in the area of the Jebel Akhdar in the interior of the country. These tribes, led by the Imam Ghalib, had retreated to the top of the Jebel where there was a fertile plateau about five miles square at a height of about 6,000 feet under the summits at 10,000 feet. The name Jebel Akhdar literally means green mountain and the name reflects the contrast between the fertility of its upper slopes and the aridity of the plains at its foot.

Brigadier Tinker, Commander LFPG, and the HQ staff of the Political Resident decided that I, as a qualified Arabist, could perhaps help solve the current problem of the whereabouts of the three leaders of the rebellion in Oman and what they were up to. It was known that they were probably in Saudi Arabia where they had considerable support and two young Omani sheikhs, loyal to the Sultan, had been persuaded to go into Saudi Arabia to find out what they could about the rebel leaders' activities and intentions. These were two young members of the ruling tribal family in Hafit immediately south of Buraimi in Omani territory. I was told by the Political Resident's staff that the two sheikhs were due to return to Hafit very soon and that I could help by going down to Sharjah, the HQ of the Trucial Oman Scouts, and thence to Buraimi where I would stay with Major Budd who commanded 'A' Squadron of the TOS. I was told that Budd would find out as soon as the sheikhs returned from Saudi Arabia so that I could go to Hafit and meet them and find out what they had learnt.

I was told that the whole plan had been agreed by London and that I was to pose as a student of archaeology from Oxford on a visit to the Trucial States to find out what archaeological possibilities there were in the area. I immediately pointed out that there was no need for such complicated subterfuge because, as a staff officer at HQ LFPG, I could simply go to Buraimi as an official visitor. The response was that the plan had been agreed by London and the political staff in Bahrain did not want to change it. I accepted that but said that at least the plan should be modified to change from Oxford, where I had never been, to Cambridge where I had in fact taken a degree. This change was also refused. Thinking this response quite crazy, but assuming that consequent problems were highly unlikely, I accepted the decision and flew down to Buraimi where I was met on the airstrip by Tim Budd. 'A' Squadron of the Scouts was quartered in the old mud fort at Buraimi (Fort Jahili) and Tim gave me the upper room in the round tower which served as the officers' quarters. There I settled down to await news of the return of the Hafit sheikhs from Saudi Arabia.

Sheikh Zayed bin Sultan and family members with Col Stewart Carter, 1960

Tim Budd and 'A' Sqn looking for water on the Qatar border

After a day or two Tim took me to see Sheikh Zayed bin Sultan who was the most important and influential sheikh of the area, recognised as such by all the local tribes in both Omani and Trucial States territories. He was the younger brother of Sheikh Shakhbut bin Sultan, the ruler of Abu Dhabi. Tim duly introduced me to Zayed as an archaeological student from Oxford and Zayed welcomed me saying that he himself was most interested in the historical sites in the area, mentioning several burial sites and ancient ruins of settlements and dams in the wadis running down from the mountains. He promised me any help I might need in my travels in the area.

The days passed and there was no news of the Hafit sheikhs until one day Tim came into the mess and said, "I've just had a signal from Sharjah and guess who is coming down here on tomorrow's Pembroke." The Pembroke was the small RAF aircraft used for a weekly run from Bahrain round the Gulf. I replied that I had no idea who might be coming, "The PR?" (The Political Resident was the senior British official in the Gulf) "No", he said, with some amusement, because he sympathised with my having had to come to Buraimi with such an unnecessary cover story, "No, our visitor is the Professor of Archaeology at Oxford University, who is coming to visit Sheikh Zayed!"

I was quite flabbergasted. This was the one man in the whole world that I just could not meet at that place and at that time. I told Tim that the only thing I could do was to vanish from Buraimi for a few days until the professor had gone. We discussed various alternatives and in the end we agreed that he should drop me at a half ruined unoccupied small house which lay in a grove of trees at the foot of the mountains about two miles away. So the next morning he duly left me with some camp kit, a jerrican of water, some food, a bottle of whisky and a good book at what turned out to be a charmingly situated hideout. He promised to visit me daily until the coast was clear for me to return. After four days of this Tim took me back to Buraimi and told me that Zayed had mentioned to the professor that one of his students was in the area and had asked Tim what had happened to me. Tim had said that he had lent me a Land Rover and that I had gone off exploring for ruined sites. Eventually the professor had departed still wondering who I was. I did not see Zayed again on that occasion and after another few days I suggested that I was wasting my time waiting for the Hafit sheikhs. HQ LFPG agreed and I went back to Bahrain. Had I known that I was to join the Scouts myself after a few months I would never have agreed to the plan as it was concocted by the FCO staff in Bahrain and London. It was some time before I could bring myself to meet Zayed again and when I did, and throughout my time in the Scouts, he always regarded me with some wry amusement, but never referred again to our first meeting.

The revolt in Oman had been going on in a desultory way for some time. The rebels had been dealt with successfully in the populated lowland areas and had retreated up into the higher valleys of the Jebel Akhdar (the green mountain) and on to its green plateau near the summit. There they were for practical purposes considered impregnable since the plateau was surrounded by steep mountainsides and cliffs up which only a few easily defended paths existed. This was the state of affairs in 1958 and it was decided that no ordinary British infantry unit could cope with the task of occupying the Jebel to end the rebellion, and that the best solution was to call in the Special Air Service Regiment to deal with the situation. 22 SAS had operated successfully in the jungles of Malaya for some years against the rebels there, but that campaign had ended and there was talk of disbanding the SAS altogether because no one could see any role for a specialist jungle unit in the future. Oman came as a golden opportunity to prove that there would continue to be suitable roles for such a unit and supporters of the SAS concept worked hard in London to get the unit sent to Oman to deal with the situation there and to prove the regiment's usefulness for the future. Thus it was that it was decided to send two squadrons of 22 SAS to Muscat in the autumn of 1958 along with the regimental HQ under Lieutenant Colonel Deane Drummond.

The HQ of the Sultan's Armed Forces in Muscat was a small affair with only about four staff officers. It was under the command of Colonel David Smiley, a well known officer of the Blues (The Royal Horse Guards) who had served in Yugoslavia during the war and had done some out of the way swashbuckling tasks in Arabia since then. It happened that the senior administrative officer at HQ SAF, Peter Middlemiss, had just gone on long mid tour leave and a replacement for him was needed to deal with the organisation of the arrival of 22 SAS in Oman and their subsequent departure. I was at that time still under-employed, to say the least, in Bahrain in HQLFPG and Brigadier Ted Tinker said he wanted to send me down to Muscat to help out in HQ SAF with the problem of looking after 22 SAS as the administrative staff officer. This I was very glad to do and arrived in Muscat in October to help plan the arrival of the visitors.

This all went fairly smoothly and a number of 3 ton vehicles and Land Rovers were shipped in together with all the other necessary equipment such as weapons and sleeping bags and so on. That and the normal Quartermaster staff function in the SAF HQ kept me fairly busy for the next few weeks.

In due course in late 1958 the SAS arrived in the shape of 'D' Squadron 22 SAS. Soon after their arrival they started patrolling up the north east side of the Jebel Akhdar up one of the few routes to the plateau. This one led up from the town of Rostaq which lay between the Jebel and the sea. At the summit of this route at the edge of the plateau there was a narrow defile along which the track lay, a place where one man with a rifle could have held the pass against a force of hundreds. There the rebels established a strong defensive position which the SAS were unable to capture and it was decided that an additional SAS squadron was needed. In early January 1959 the commander of 22 SAS, Lieutenant Colonel Deane Drummond, along with his tactical HQ and 'A' Squadron 22 SAS arrived in Oman and operational planning began. It had become obvious that the key to taking the Jebel was surprise. When they arrived 'A' Squadron relieved 'D' Squadron which redeployed to the south west of the Jebel.

There were only two or three hundred rebels on the Jebel and only three or four feasible tracks up the mountain, all of which were fairly easily defended, so a successful assault was impossible without an element of complete surprise. The essence of Colonel Deane Drummond's plan was to make a concentration of forces on one side of the mountain and then suddenly to switch an assault force by night to the other side and go up the mountain the same night, not up one of the existing routes, but straight up one of the steep sides between the known tracks.

Tactical HQ was at Nizwa, a town at the foot of the Jebel on the south western side on the edge of the desert. This was where Deane Drummond finalised his plan. I was with him and his staff when he was going over the plan for the operation one day when he suddenly said, "We need some artillery support. We have a troop of guns but no gunner officer. You're a gunner, Tony, what sort of a gunner are you?" I said, "Well, I started off as a mountain gunner and then was an airborne gunner and a field gunner. Why?" He said, "Then you're just the chap to command the SAF artillery troop and to come up the jebel with me as FOO (Forward Observation Officer) to give us some gunner support if required." I said, "OK sir, but what makes you think that I'm capable of going up that mountain with you lot?" At which his reply was, "Because you're a British officer, that's why!" I could not think of an answer to that so set about planning the artillery support for the operation.

I had a minor problem then as I had no kit for such an operation, but the SAS stores soon fitted me out with a bergen rucksack and a pair of their mountain boots. I mentioned the problem of wearing the boots in with only a few days to go at which the quartermaster sergeant gave me some very useful advice. This was to soak the new boots overnight in a bucket of water, put them on straight out of the bucket in the morning and then walk them in over a distance until they were dry. That I did and it worked like a charm. I had no problem with my feet or with blisters for the whole operation. The other problem was to get ready to carry a bergen full of various kit and two days rations and a large wireless battery, weighing altogether about 60 lbs, up a mountain side for a height of about 5,000 feet. The only thing I could do by way of preparation was to fill the bergen with stones and go out daily, scrambling up and down the foothills for an hour or two. It was surprising how soon one got used to the weight.

The next thing was to go and talk to the people at the guns. At that time there were no gunner officers in Oman except me, but at the gun position there were two senior warrant officers seconded from the Pakistan Army and under them the guns were manned by locally trained gunners. The essence of artillery fire support in army operations lies in two factors, speed in correcting the fall of shot on to the target and accuracy in hitting it, but another important factor is the need for simplicity in fire control procedures. To simplify work at the OP (the forward observation post) the Royal Artillery at home had long before changed their system of fire orders from the OP to the gun position from 'line of fire' procedure to a target grid system. This change made the job of the FOO at the OP much simpler but it required additional careful paperwork at the gun position.[1]

When I discussed the problems at the gun position with the Pakistani WOs it became apparent that they had no great faith in the accuracy of the work of the Omani command post staff in dealing with target grid

---

1. The change from 'line of fire procedure' to 'target grid procedure' was done to make things simpler at the OP, so that anyone, whether or not trained in gunnery techniques, can control the guns and engage targets. Traditionally the FOO visualised the line on the ground from the guns to the target and made corrections with reference to that line. With the target grid system the FOO gives his corrections with reference to the line from his position to the target, no matter where the gun position is. But this requires some slightly complicated procedures at the gun position which makes the response from the guns slower. It also uses more ammunition to range on to a target. With the line of fire system the FOO's corrections could go straight and unaltered to the guns without any input from the command post at the gun position, a simpler and quicker procedure.

corrections. I asked them whether they would prefer it if I reverted to the old 'line of fire' system of fire control corrections and they seized on that idea with great relief because, as they told me, if I had used target grid procedure they would have had to do all the command post work themselves, whereas 'line of fire' corrections from the OP could be passed straight to the guns without any adjustment. So it happened that for the first time for years I was able to return to the old fast and simple system.

There remained the question of the artillery fire plan to be worked out by me in conjunction with the SAS operation planners. All this had to be done off aerial photos of the mountain because the available maps were so rudimentary. Finally there was the question of communications between the FOO and the guns. For many years the standard method in the British service had been by voice over the wireless link. This had long ago superseded fire orders by the use of wireless telegraphy and the Morse code, but the trouble was that the use of voice communications was of questionable effectiveness in the mountains. W/T and morse would be far more reliable, but I was trained in neither. By great good fortune however, there was a British Royal Signals corporal in Nizwa who happened to have been trained in W/T and, moreover, in artillery fire orders procedure using morse. He happily volunteered to join me as my OP assistant and signaller and with him on board the gunner support for the operation was as well organised as I could make it. The corporal carried the wireless set in his bergen and I carried the batteries. The guns available were two 5.5 inch medium guns, two 25 pounder field guns and two 75mm light guns, all at a gun position east of Nizwa.

Just before D day in late January 1959 'A' squadron from above Rostaq marched round the northern side of the Jebel to Tarif on the western side and then at dusk on D day they got into their three tonners and were driven round to the assembly point at the foot of the Jebel near Nizwa on the other side of the mountain from Rostaq. There they joined up with the commanding officer and 'D' Squadron. This force then started up the mountain up the steep slabs of rock between two of the well known wadi tracks up the Jebel which lay on either side. I, as the gunner FOO, went up with Deane Drummond after the first squadron.

We knew that the rebels had a heavy machine gun post at a strategic point commanding the two valleys that lay one on each side of our route. We hoped to surprise this post and silence it quickly, and in this the leading squadron succeeded. The three men manning the gun were fast asleep in a cave and were easily and quietly dealt with. Up to that point the route had been a long slog up the steeply sloping rock, but there had been no need to use one's hands except occasionally to keep one's balance. At one point the route lay along a ledge across a short cliff face and the leading squadron fixed ropes along the difficult bit and that was fairly easily traversed. Finally the leading squadron reached the ridge at the edge of the plateau and we took up a defensive position along it.

A dismounted troop of the Life Guards, which was stationed at Sharjah near Dubai, had followed the SAS squadrons up the Jebel and was in a defensive position to our left. I was asked to register some targets to defend their position and this I proceeded to do. By this time both the 25 pounders and the 75mm guns were out of range, partly because of the distance we had come and partly because of the fact that we were now some 4,000 feet higher than the gun position. However, the 5.5s could still make it and I successfully ranged in on the targets. After that the Life Guards remained on the first ridge and consolidated the position while the SAS squadrons moved on to the next ridge on the plateau. There we were confronted with a valley and beyond it a steep hill with a cave mouth near the top occupied by a number of rebels who were firing at anyone who moved forward from the second ridge which we were on. At that stage Deane Drummond told me he would like support from the guns to get the rebels out of the cave. This was a typical mountain gunnery problem in that the cave was near the top of a steep hill on a third ridge and there was a fairly steep valley between it and our position. Furthermore I suspected that there was a deep valley on the other side of it which meant that ranging on to the target presented unusual problems, especially as the maps I had were rudimentary and the aerial photos gave very little idea of the contours of the ground. This meant that ranging rounds were very likely to fall in some steep valley invisible to the forward observer. However, I was lucky enough before too long to get a round on to the steep slope below the cave and then another just below its entrance. At that, the half dozen or so rebels burst out of the cave and fled up the hill and disappeared over the top.

Years later I have noticed that the official MoD (British Ministry of Defence) account of the SAS Jebel Akhdar operation makes no mention of artillery support, except to say that a donkey was allocated to the FOO to carry his wireless set! I don't know how far back the donkeys were, but I don't recollect seeing any on the Jebel and the MoD account specifically mentions that the donkeys could not negotiate the climb beyond the halfway point, so the FOO party would have been quite useless if it had not carried its own wireless equipment. There are few things of less use than an FOO with no communications.

As it turned out that was the end of rebel resistance at our end of the plateau and the advance of the SAS squadrons to the small cluster of villages on that part of the plateau, Habib, Shuraija and Saiq, was unopposed. I stayed with Deane Drummond for two or three days in case more fire support was needed, but it became obvious that it would not be necessary. At that stage Deane Drummond said that his own communications had broken down and that, in view of the fact that artillery support was no longer required, he wished to commandeer my signaller and my set. This was in those days a not unheard of situation between the gunners and the infantry, whose communications quite often used to fail!

So I decided that there wasn't much point in my staying on top of the Jebel any longer since there was nothing more I could contribute to the operation and I had a lot of staff work to get on with down below. So, with Deane Drummond's permission, I set off the next day down the Wadi Kamah track. This was downhill nearly all the way and my bergen was very much lighter than it had been on the way up, which made it a pleasant contrast. I was overtaken by nightfall about halfway down and bedded down next to a little shrine by the path. Despite the cold night air I had a very comfortably warm night, the reason for which became obvious in the morning, when I saw that I had put my sleeping bag down on to a soft flat area of donkey dung which retained the warmth of the midday sun and also probably was warmed by some degree of internal fermentation. Obviously men and donkeys had broken their journeys up and down the mountain at that point for many years.

The next day was a pleasant stroll all downhill to the entrance to the Wadi Kamah, not far from the point from which we had initially set off up the mountain. So ended my short operational stint with the SAS. I only had one real shoot, but I do think that the sudden arrival of a few 100lb shells was probably a not insignificant factor in causing the rebels to flee off the jebel. The leaders fled to Saudi Arabia and the tribesmen, on being told that no further action would be taken against them if they surrendered their weapons, did so and returned to their villages.

I returned to HQ SAF in Muscat and got on with arranging the 'Q' side of the return of the SAS to the UK. For political reasons they had to be out of the country by the end of March and they filled in the intervening time by patrolling in troop strength up and down all the few tracks up the Jebel

Akhdar, accompanied by SAF representatives to show the flag and to demonstrate that the Sultan was again in control of the country. When the SAS had departed I took a convoy of their Land Rovers and 3 ton Bedford trucks, which had been allotted to the Trucial Oman Scouts, by land north to their HQ at Sharjah.

This was not an enjoyable journey. The drivers of the vehicles were SAS personnel and not familiar with the local driving conditions. They were all right on gravel tracks, but not on soft sand and soft beaches. In those days the drive from Muscat to Sharjah was along the Batinah coast to the north and then inland through a gap in the mountains, the Wadi Qawr, to the coastal plain of the Trucial States and to the sea at Sharjah. The Batinah coast was lined with palm groves and fishing villages every few miles. The main track led through the palm groves parallel to the shore and in winter was muddy and rough and often washed away in places. So it was very slow and uncomfortable. The solution was to drive along the beach at low tide and that was comparatively comfortable and much faster, but could be difficult. Earlier that winter a titled young officer of the Life Guards had managed to get his ferret scout car stuck in the sand with the tide coming in. When the tide had come in and gone out again all one could see of the scout car was the ring on the top of its turret. It was a very difficult task to get it on to dry land and then it had to be shipped back to the UK as the repairs needed were quite beyond the local army facilities.

So I decided to take the beach route at low tide, but with a very careful briefing of the drivers beforehand. All went well until we got about halfway along the coastal stretch of the route to a fishing village called Shinas. This village was right on the edge of the sea and at high tide there was only a steep strip of soft sand about five yards wide between the village wall and the water. At low tide there was a wider strip of fairly hard sand which offered a good route past the village if one took it at a reasonable pace and did not on any account stop. The alternative at this point was a long detour inland. So I got the drivers together and told them that they must without fail get into four wheel drive while they were still on hard ground, then go down the soft sand slope at a good speed which they must keep up on the hard sand past the village, so that they could take a good run at the soft sand slope the other side of the village to get up on to hard ground again. I said two or three times that it was essential to be in four wheel drive and the correct gear from the very start, as any gear changing during the crossing could be disastrous.

All went well at first and all the Land Rovers got through. Then came the three tonners. The first three made it well and then came the fourth which went down the soft slope and on to the harder sand well enough, but at that point the driver attempted a gear change, and at that his rear wheels began to spin while the front ones did not turn, making it obvious that he was not even in four wheel drive. The vehicle slowly settled down on to its axles. That would not have been too great a problem for a normal army unit with a full complement of officers, NCOs and men, but I only had myself and a dozen drivers with no experience of getting out a vehicle stuck in sand, and the tide was on the turn. It was a long struggle and we were overtaken by the tide and by darkness while we laboured. While we were all digging away the sand I realised that, in accordance with local custom, this beach was in fact used as the public lavatory for the whole village. Most of what was deposited on its surface was washed away daily by the sea, but enough remained behind just under the surface of the sand to make our digging a most unpleasant experience. Fortunately the vehicle was not as far down the beach as the scout car must have been and the tide did not come up over its engine. So in the end, when the tide had gone out again, we managed to get it on to dry land and the convoy proceeded on its way.

There was one other incident before we finally got to Sharjah when one of the three tonners got stuck in the sand. This was dry sand and part of a sand dune which lay across the track. This time a three tonner belonging to the Trucial Oman Scouts happened to appear with two bedouin drivers who offered assistance. The SAS drivers had been digging away without success, fortunately not for very long, and one of the Scouts' drivers hopped up into the cab and, after a little deft soft sand type driving, got the vehicle out on to hard ground in a trice. After that it was easy going into Sharjah and the Scouts' main camp.

CHAPTER 4

The Trucial Oman Scouts 1959–1961

While I was on the Jebel Akhdar at the end of the SAS operation I met Colonel Stewart Carter, the commander of the Trucial Oman Scouts. He was on the Jebel to visit 'C' Squadron of the Scouts which was in support of the SAS for the operation. He asked me what I was doing and, on hearing my explanation about why I had been sent down temporarily from Bahrain to Muscat, said he was looking for a staff officer to be seconded to the Scouts to act as Brigade Major and asked me if I would like the job. I took to Stewart Carter immediately and said I would very much like the job, so he said he would fix the posting as soon as he got back to Sharjah.

Stewart Carter was an imposing figure, who resembled Stalin in looks! He had had a colourful career, latterly as commander of the Hong Kong Defence Force, and had been posted into the Scouts to get the unit on to a more professional footing than it had been on up to that time and to enlarge it to cope with its widening role. He was revered by everyone and was a wonderful man to work for.

*Colonel Stewart Carter, Commander
Trucial Oman Scouts, 1960*

The Scouts had played a major part in finally evicting the Saudis from Buraimi in 1955. Then, after a short respite, they had found themselves increasingly stretched to cope with their various responsibilities. In the summer of 1957 the rebels in Oman had managed to overrun a number of villages to the south and west of the Jebel Akhdar and inflicted a serious defeat on the Omani forces opposing them. The Sultan appealed to the British for help in defeating the rebels and a force was quickly put together under Stewart Carter in the area of Fahud some sixty miles south west of Nizwa. This consisted of the TOS Tactical HQ, three Scouts squadrons, a company of the Cameronians, a troop of the 15th/19th Hussars and elements of the Omani Northern Frontier Regiment. The force advanced against the rebels and, one by one, retook the villages which hastily struck the Imam's white flag and hoisted the Sultan's red flag in its place. After a few days they finally secured the town of Nizwa and the campaign was over, with the rebels fleeing up the Jebel to their lair on the seemingly impregnable plateau 5,000ft above the surrounding plain. So the Scouts had played a major part in the Nizwa campaign against the rebels who were fighting for an Imamate in the hills of Oman independent of the Sultan in Muscat. At the same time they had remained responsible for peace and security in the Trucial States. Then in 1958 and early 1959 the Scouts had made an important contribution to the final operation in which 22 SAS finally conquered the Jebel.

After their defeat on the Jebel in January 1959 the rebel leaders escaped from the area and found their way back to Dammam in Saudi Arabia. From there Talib, the rebel military leader, with Saudi help and support, organised a campaign against the Sultan's Armed Forces and the oil company in Oman. This was based on mining the roads and tracks and destroying as many vehicles as possible. The mines used were American and increasingly powerful ones were smuggled into Oman through the Trucial States by a variety of means. Regularly, week by week, vehicles were destroyed and their occupants often wounded or killed by these mines. Countering this campaign was one of the main tasks of the Scouts for a long period. This required constant patrolling of all the possible smuggling routes through the sheikhdoms and the searching of all the traffic encountered by the patrols whether by vehicle, camel or donkey. At the same time much effort was expended on intelligence gathering to find out who the smugglers were, the identity of their sympathisers and the routes that were being used. There was considerable sympathy with the rebel cause in some of the hill tribes and there was a constant supply of

35

One of the main highways in the Trucial States, 1960

A typical camel train on a main highway track in the Trucial States, 1960

minelayers and mine smugglers due to that residual tribal loyalty and to the amounts of money on offer to those who took part in the campaign.

I was never blown up on a mine, but I remember a big training exercise in Omani territory well south of Buraimi involving the Scouts, SAF and the SAS, during which the Scouts HQ were travelling down a wide desert track and the Scouts medical officer behind me hit a mine in his Land Rover and was thrown up through the canvas roof of the vehicle and landed some yards away in the sand. He was shaken and most annoyed, but was unhurt. His vehicle was destroyed.

The area for which the Scouts were responsible included the seven sheikhdoms of the Trucial States, so called because of the maritime truce imposed on them many years before. On the departure of the British from the Gulf in 1971 these sheikhdoms would become the United Arab Emirates and so remain today. However, when the Scouts were initially formed, as the Trucial Oman Levies, Oman had virtually no army and the border between Oman and the Trucial Sheikhdoms was not only undemarcated on the ground, but also only very vaguely marked on the then rudimentary maps.

Two of the Buraimi oases in 1960

Thus it was that the Scouts, when I joined them, still had security responsibilities in Oman north and west of Muscat and regularly patrolled the areas south east of Buraimi to Nizwa in Oman and thence through the Wadi Sumail to Muscat. The way back led north west up the Oman coast and back to Sharjah. The Scouts squadrons and their patrols were accepted everywhere as the embryonic local army and fulfilled a function which would have needed a regular British force of ten times the size of the Scouts if the policy had been to maintain security in the area that way.

It was plain that in the immediate future an expansion and reorganisation of the Scouts was required in order to continue to provide active patrolling in all the Trucial States to maintain security and, at the same time, to be able to take the field as a well organised force to deal with any rebel activity in their area. It might also be necessary to deploy such a force in the territory of the Sultanate for as long as the Sultan's Armed Forces remained too weak to cope with such a thing on their own. So a new establishment was approved which expanded the staff at TOS HQ and provided a mobile regiment of three squadrons under the command of a lieutenant-colonel in addition to three patrol squadrons. Hence the decision to appoint a brigade major, effectively a chief of staff, together with an administrative staff officer to the HQ. The latter turned out to be Gerry Charrington of the 9/12th Lancers.

Tony Cawston at the Scouts' HQ Sharjah 1960

The essence of the task of the Scouts therefore required constant patrolling on foot, by vehicle or by camel. Land Rovers were used wherever possible, but they could not cope with the soft sand dunes in the Liwa to the west of the area, nor with some of the camel trails in the hills in places where they were too narrow for a vehicle. There was a constant administrative battle for the supply of the necessary equipment and vehicles to cope with soft sand. The first thing was sand tyres which made a big difference, but on any journey away from Scouts camps each vehicle had to carry two jerricans of water and three of petrol, in addition to the floor being covered with half filled sandbags as a measure of protection against mines, so there was only room for three people with the necessary kit in one vehicle. The point was that, if a vehicle broke down, it had to be repaired on the spot or to remain where it was until retrieved and the crew had to remain with it. This meant there had to be plenty of water which was vital, particularly in the heat of summer. The extra petrol was needed because, as there were no tarmac roads in the whole area except three miles

Abu Dhabi in 1960. The view on entry to the island. Sheikh Shakhbut's palace to the left

Dubai and its creek from the air in 1960

of tarmac near Muscat, all the roads were gravel and rock tracks with sandy patches, and Land Rovers ran in four wheel drive and 2nd or 3rd gear for much of any journey, so one could only do four or five miles to the gallon at best. When British units operated in the area the drinking water required was laid down as one jerrican (4.5 gallons) per day per head, but we made do with rather less. Even so the load was considerable for a Land Rover and in soft sand the engine was not powerful enough to cope, so we asked for some better vehicles for the task. The oil companies used Dodge Power Wagons which I had had in the Indian Army and had found unstoppable, and we asked for those, but they were American and expensive and so we were sent a couple of British one ton vehicles with four wheel drive for trials, one a Morris I remember, but neither had the requisite power. In the end some Dodges were supplied.

The deployment of Scouts squadrons depended on what was going on in the various tribal areas. From time to time tribal disputes arose which threatened to get out of hand and develop into tribal warfare. When such a problem occurred, a Scouts patrol would be sent to the area to restore calm and seek a solution to the problem, which was probably concerning access to a well or to an area used for the collection of firewood. Scouts officers became adept at devising solutions acceptable to both sides and the appearance of a few Scouts soldiers had a calming effect. In particular, in my time the presence of Major Jim Stockdale was considered to be worth a squadron of Scouts in such a situation.

A typical situation of this sort arose in 1959 when the inhabitants of Asimah and Tayyiba came to blows over a land boundary dispute and some people were killed in the ensuing exchange of rifle fire. These two villages were on the border between Ras al Khaimah and Fujairah, both of which had territories split in two and intertwined with each other in the fertile hill country south of the Musandam. Sheikh Mohammed of Fujairah always seemed to be the odd man out in the development of the Trucial States. His sheikhdom was the only one entirely on the Indian Ocean coast, although Sharjah did have three enclaves there too. He often accused Sheikh Saqr of Ras al Khaimah of buying up property in Fujairah and relations between the two were never good. The problem on their mutual border was complicated by conflicting tribal loyalties in the two villages and this led to the shooting. 'C' Squadron under John Pott was immediately sent to restore order and its arrival quickly quietened the situation. The Political Agent became involved in arbitrating a settlement.

The location of the Scouts squadrons changed from time to time over the years as the security situation in the various tribal areas changed and as oil company requirements concerning the protection of their prospecting or drilling parties altered. There was usually a squadron based in Sharjah in addition to the Scouts HQ squadron and usually one at Fort Jahili at Al Ain, one of the villages belonging to Abu Dhabi in the Buraimi oasis area. But in any case, in order to keep the squadrons on their toes and ready to move at any time, there was a periodic exercise known as 'Roundabout' under which squadrons rotated every few months from camp to camp. This helped to prevent personal relationships between Scouts soldiers and local civilians developing into anything too close or potentially subversive.

It also ensured that the various camp sites, some pleasant and some not so pleasant, should be shared on an equitable basis. For instance in 1960 a

The fort at Buraimi, Jahili, 1960

The squadron camp site at Mirfa, 150 miles SW of Sharjah, 1960

The Scouts' training centre, Manama, 1960. An Arab officer in the foreground

squadron was based at Mirfa about half way along the coast between Sharjah and Qatar. This was necessary for the security of the oil company which had a camp nearby from which prospecting operations and drilling were being carried out. It was a desolate and unpleasant area with no nearby village, surrounded to the north by the flat shallow waters of the southern Gulf and to the south by flat featureless desert composed largely of treacherous salt flats. It was subject to extremes of heat and humidity in summer and the squadron lived there under canvas with, of course, no such thing as air conditioning. At the other end of the scale was the camp at Fort Jahili at Al Ain. Here there was civilisation and mud brick buildings to live in. There were nearby villages and date gardens and the climate was dry air which was seldom too hot for comfort. The squadron at Mirfa always looked forward to 'Roundabout', but particularly if it meant a move to Jahili.

My tour in the Scouts lasted from March '59 to early '61, just under two years, and was one of the most fulfilling periods of my service. When I arrived in Sharjah the Scouts consisted of an HQ, four squadrons, 'A', 'B', 'C', and 'D' and a training squadron. Another squadron, 'X' squadron, was formed soon afterwards and, as already mentioned, the plan was to form some of the squadrons into a desert regiment. The Scouts as a unit was not large. It numbered about 30 British officers, 20 Arab officers, 40 British NCOs and 1300 Arab other ranks. Scouts officers came from all parts of the army and had very varied backgrounds. The British were all regulars seconded from the British Army and, unlike SAF in Oman, there were no contract personnel. The Scouts were considered by the Ministry of Defence and by the HQ in Aden to be subject to the Army Act and to British Army discipline and military law. They were the last unit in the Empire in which this was the case. The view of the Political Resident in Bahrain and the Political Agent in Dubai supported by the Foreign Office was somewhat different. They considered that the TOS as a unit was subject to local political constraints and that it should be run independently by its commander under the authority of the PR with minimal interference from the HQ in Aden. This difference of views affected policy making throughout my time and this argument particularly affected the formation of the Desert Regiment and the enlargement of the TOS HQ. The military view was that the expansion of the Scouts was important for two reasons, first in order to enable the TOS to perform their dual function of maintaining security in the Trucial States whilst being able to provide a force of one or two squadrons to assist the SAF in Oman when required and, secondly, to provide a brigade HQ in the event of British troops being deployed in the area if an emergency so required.

In due course the formation of the Desert Regiment went ahead and a lieutenant colonel was posted in as its CO. This was Bill Bowen of the Worcestershires. The regiment was formed and was stationed in the Buraimi area with the Jahili squadron, which was 'C' Squadron and with 'X' Squadron of Dhofaris under Ken Wilson. But there was disagreement over the wisdom of reinforcing the Scouts' presence in such a politically sensitive area and the view prevailed that the Desert Regiment should move elsewhere, so it was reformed with 'A' and 'D' Squadrons joining 'X' Squadron at Manama to the north. This left 'B' Squadron under Ian Craig Adams at Mirfa. Very soon after I left the Scouts decisions were taken which were based on the final recognition that the Scouts would never again operate in Oman, except to some degree in the Dhahira, south of Buraimi. This latter exception was based on the fact that the British had found it very difficult to persuade the Sultan to take any interest in the area and that, regardless of the boundary between Abu Dhabi and Oman, Sheikh Zayed of Abu Dhabi was regarded as the most influential sheikh of the region on both sides of the border. Another factor was the recognition that the British element in the Scouts had become too great, in particular in the case of the NCOs. The upshot was that the Desert Regiment was disbanded and the Scouts returned to their former organisation.

The Dhofaris of 'X' Squadron produced special problems. They were warlike people and excellent soldiers and the squadron commander, Ken Wilson, thought the world of them, but they were native to the southern coastal region of Oman and were foreigners in the Trucial States. Special rules had to be applied when they went home on leave to prevent them taking their weapons with them and never coming back. As mountain people they were especially useful in the hills, more useful than the bedu soldiers, men of the desert who excelled in the sandy wastes. The same differences applied concerning the Beni Ka'ab, the other mountain people who joined the Scouts. They too were Omanis, but came from the normal Scouts area of operations near Buraimi and their sheikh, Abdullah bin Salim, we regarded as on a par with the seven Rulers of the Trucial States and as a very good friend.

I used to travel from Sharjah to Buraimi and Al Ain and back fairly frequently and there were two routes in use at the time. The shorter and more direct one involved crossing an area of large sand dunes which could be awkward when conditions were not favourable, particularly in summer.

45

The shorter route over the sands from Buraimi to Sharjah, 1960

The longer route via Mahadha from Buraimi to Sharjah

The longer route, reliable in all weathers, led north up a long wadi bed to Mahadha and then in a north westerly direction along a gravel track avoiding the large sand dunes to Sharjah. Mahadha was Abdullah bin Salim's home town and was in fact in Omani territory, but there were no border posts in those days and one travelled in and out of Oman without noticing any border at all. I used to break my journey frequently at Mahadha to call on Sheikh Abdullah in his fort there. That was always an enjoyable interlude.

Once, when I broke my journey in Mahadha intending to call on Abdullah, I found that he was away and I always remember his wife, veiled and dressed in black, standing very erect above me on one of the towers of the fort, giving me a most friendly greeting and explaining that she was alone in the building, with Sheikh Abdullah away, the implication being that therefore she was very sorry but she could not let me in. I have always thought that that picture summed up the admirable social attitudes of Omani society based on several thousand years of civilisation. At that time evidence of an ancient city was being discovered in Bahrain and since then similar discoveries have been made on the coast very near Abu Dhabi and again near Ras al Khaimah.

Sheikh Abdullah bin Salim al Ka'abi

Another incident, which to me was symbolic of the strength and cohesion of Omani tribal society based on centuries of history, occurred just after the Jebel Akhdar campaign before the SAS had left the country. One of the SAS officers whom I had got to know quite well came to me and said, "You know, Tony, that I and my wife Antonia do a lot of climbing. Well, Antonia is at the moment with a mountaineering party in the Himalayas and next week is our wedding anniversary. We promised each other that on that day we would each get up to the highest point in whatever country we happened to be in and then drink to each other's health up there. I would very much like your help in doing this next week." I said, "By all means. I'm no climber, but the highest point in Oman is the Jebel Sham at the northwestern end of the Jebel Akhdar massif, and it's a long, steep, but simple walk to the top which is at about 10,000 feet. I will take a couple of days off and come with you." So I made enquiries about which tribal area was concerned and found that the Sheikh of Bahlah at the foot of the Jebel was recognised as being the tribal leader in the area. It was customary for anyone from outside a tribal area to seek permission from the local sheikh before travelling within it. This ensured that the traveller would be protected from molestation in that tribal area. So I went to Bahlah and found the sheikh's house. I was told that he would shortly be in his majlis, the traditional Arab tribal leader's meeting place in which members of the tribe have personal access to their sheikh. I was told that I should wait there until he came. I was shown into a large room in which several tribesmen were sitting round the walls with their rifles, one or two with falcons on their wrists. The one who looked the eldest indicated that I should sit next to him, so I did, and told him what I had come for. He said that it was a simple matter and we would be very welcome, but I should formally ask the sheikh for his permission. He said that the sheikh had in fact gone to Muscat to see the Sultan but that his son would arrive shortly to deputise for his father in whatever business arose in the majlis that day. So I sat waiting and talking to my neighbours until there was a stir in the room and I was told the sheikh's son was about to arrive. Then with great dignity a young boy of about twelve or thirteen entered the room and sat down at the head of the room and motioned to me to come and sit beside him. There followed a pleasant conversation in which I explained why I had come and asked his permission to take a small party up to the top of his mountain. He agreed to that in a most gracious manner and offered guides and food and donkeys all of which I politely declined and after a further exchange of good wishes took my leave. The boy was most affable and authoritative throughout and everyone treated him exactly as they would have treated his father. To me it was a graphic illustration of the strength and cohesion of the Omani tribal system. He did not have what we in the West would call a good education, but at his young age he was already fitted to fill the role of tribal leader which would be his in the future.

The Dhofari problem is illustrated by an event that occurred while 'X' Squadron happened to be in Sharjah and Ken Wilson was living in the HQ mess. I had noticed that Ken's Land Rover had been parked near my room at night and had then disappeared and I had thought nothing of it. Then I heard that Ken's driver had disappeared, no one knew where. Finally Ken found that his Land Rover was missing. His driver had told him that he had taken it into the workshop for some repair but when Ken asked when it would be ready for collection the workshop said they had never received it. And then enquiries revealed that the missing driver had driven down to Muscat and sold the vehicle there. We managed to get the man arrested and accused of theft so Ken was told to go down to Muscat to give evidence in court and to bring the vehicle back. There was then a delay of a few days before the case came to court and we thought that all was well, but Ken arrived back in Sharjah and reported that the judge had asked him to give evidence on oath. Then, on finding that Ken was Christian, he ruled that no evidence was acceptable from him in that Shari'a court and dismissed the case. We protested in vain through the embassy and through friends in SAF, but nothing could be done.

During my time in Sharjah the senior representative of the British Government was the Political Agent Trucial States who reported to the Political Resident Persian Gulf in Bahrain. When I arrived in Scouts HQ the PA was Donald Hawley who, during my time and later, did an immense amount to bring the seven Rulers together in their thinking about the future and their acceptance of the idea and the advantages of forming a union of the sheikhdoms leading up to eventual independence. He had originally served in the Sudan Defence Force and had then transferred to the Sudan Political Service for a number of years, often in a judicial capacity being a member of the Bar. I gathered all this during one of my first routine meetings with him and I asked him which Inn of Court he had joined. He replied that he was a member of the Inner Temple and I remarked that I was a member too. He asked when I had been 'called' and I had to confess that I had funked getting myself called although I was fully qualified because I, due to my age, was almost certain to have to make the speech at dinner on call night in reply to that of the presiding senior bencher. "Whyever was that?" said Donald. "Because I have heard several of the speeches given on those occasions and they are all so erudite and so impressively larded with Greek and Latin quotations that I have so far decided that I cannot compete!" I said. Donald then told me in the nicest way that I was a complete coward and that in fact it would be most refreshing on call night for someone to get up and make a different sort of speech and that my army service should supply me with plenty of subject matter to do that. So he shamed me there and then to declare that I would get 'called' as soon as I could.

I then made arrangements to attend an appropriate 'call' night during my next leave and was duly told that I was the senior student and should prepare a speech. However, before I had done more than thinking about the problem from time to time, the Secretary at the Inner Temple wrote to tell me that an even more senior student was being called on the same night, that he was Minister of Justice in the Indian state of Uttar Pradesh, and that he had therefore been deputed to make the speech. So I awaited the occasion with equanimity. At the dinner I found myself sitting at one of the usual foursome tables opposite one of the most beautiful girls I have ever seen. She came from northern Nigeria and was very dark with handsome aquiline features. I found myself talking to her for most of the dinner. I couldn't get much of a response from either of the other two at the table, but it was noticeable that the man on my right, who looked to me to be Indian, was in a highly nervous state.

In due course the meal ended and the senior bencher presiding made a somewhat perfunctory speech of welcome and sat down. After a pause, my Indian neighbour rather shakily got to his feet and said, "On behalf of student body, thank you very much." And he sat down and that was that! Donald Hawley was quite amused when I told him the story.

As already mentioned, the commander of 'C' Squadron was John Pott who had taken part in the airborne operation at Arnhem in 1944, famous later for being 'a bridge too far'. He was also one of the Scouts officers who had served in the Sudan Defence Force. I remember visiting his squadron and the training centre one day and being told that he had taken a patrol out to deal with another fracas that was taking place between two villages on the border between two sheikhdoms over competing claims over a well in their vicinity. John was highly respected in the area around Manama and had a reputation for successfully defusing such situations which were not uncommon in the more populated parts of the fertile areas in the

Major John Pott, OC 'C' Squadron, 1960

foothills of the main mountain chain. He came into the squadron mess tent while I was there for a hurried bite of lunch, which consisted of a tinful of sardines, eaten out of the tin with a fork, before jumping into his Land Rover again to go back to the villages where the sheikhs concerned were awaiting his mediation in their dispute. A day or two later his report arrived in the Sharjah HQ saying that the dispute had been successfully resolved and all was peace again. It was a very typical example of the Scouts contribution to the building of what was to become the unified UAE. John finally retired to Scotland where he continued to make occasional parachute jumps for charity until late in life.

It was Stewart Carter's policy to bring on suitable young soldiers to become officers and one of these in my time was Faisal bin Sultan al Qassimi, a member of the ruling family of Ras al Khaimah. Initially these young officers were locally commissioned and were the equivalent of the VCOs in the Indian Army and Faisal spent some time in that rank as an officer training soldiers in Sharjah. Then the outstanding ones were sent to the UK to the Mons Officer Cadet School in order to become Trucial States commissioned officers, on the same level as the British officers. Faisal went through Mons in my time and returned to become second in command of a squadron in due course.

Unfortunately, when the Arab-Israel war broke out in 1967, he, along with some others, felt he could no longer serve alongside the British in the Scouts and he resigned. A few years later, when I had left the army and was visiting Abu Dhabi with the party from the British Aircraft Corporation who were promoting the sale of Rapier, there was Faisal as a general commanding the Abu Dhabi Defence Force. It was very pleasing to see that he had done so well in the military service of his country.

CHAPTER 5

The Scouts – Some lighter moments

When I first joined the Scouts and for some time thereafter the Intelligence Officer at Scouts' HQ was Peter Chubb. He was responsible for gathering information on what was going on in the Trucial States and for maintaining good relations with the Rulers of the seven sheikhdoms, Abu Dhabi, Dubai, Sharjah, Ajman, Umm al Quwain, Ras al Khaimah and Fujairah. When Peter Chubb left the Scouts at the end of his tour the job of IO devolved on to me for a time as the remaining Arabic speaker in the HQ at Sharjah. It was during this time that Sheikh Rashid, the Ruler of Ajman, was invited to London on a state visit and it fell to me to keep in touch with him as the travel arrangements were made. Rashid was an elderly man of most imposing presence with a magnificent wide and long white beard which came right down to his waist and beyond. I called on him several times to tell him about the arrangements and at one point mentioned that he would fly to Bahrain and then take an aircraft that would take him through to Heathrow, but that it would stop at Rome to refuel.

Major Peter Chubb, Scouts' intelligence officer

Sheikh Rashid bin Humaid of Ajman, 1960

At that he said, "Will I be able to meet the British governor of Italy?" I replied that Rome had been an empire, but very long ago, long before the existence of the British Empire, and that it was now an independent country, with which we British had friendly relations and we maintained an embassy there with a senior ambassador whose staff would be pleased to sort out any problems Rashid might encounter at Rome, but that the need for such assistance would be very unlikely. He seemed disappointed at this and gave me the impression that he did not really believe what I had said about the then state of the British Empire in the area. I reported the conversation to the people at the HQ in Bahrain, HQ Land Forces Persian Gulf, and later duly saw Shaikh Rashid off at the airfield at Sharjah on his way to London.

We heard that the visit had gone well and that Rashid had seemed well pleased. A week or two later the staff in Bahrain asked me to go and see Rashid to find out what he had thought, on reflection, of his visit and whether any points had arisen which we should bear in mind when other Rulers were invited to London. So I drove out to Ajman and was received cordially by Rashid in his majlis. He expressed great satisfaction at how the visit had gone and how pleased and honoured he had been to be received by the Queen and then, with a twinkle in his eye, said, "I knew you were pulling my leg when you told me the other day that Rome was not part of the British Empire and that there was no British governor there". I was a bit nonplussed at that and asked him what he meant and what had happened at Rome. He replied, "Well, we landed at Rome and I was told that there was no time for people to get off the aircraft while it was refuelled, but that there was an Englishman who had come down to talk to me on the plane. And there he was, your British governor, who had come to the airport specially to talk to me. He spoke very good Arabic and we had a most enjoyable chat, so don't you try and put over such stories about the British Empire to me again!" I thought it best just to laugh and leave it at that, at least for the moment.

I reported all this to HQLFPG and asked what had in fact happened at Rome. The answer was that apparently the FCO had sent a telegram to the embassy in Rome telling them that Rashid was coming on an aircraft to Rome for refuelling on his way to London and suggesting that, if there were an Arabic speaker in the embassy, it would be a nice gesture if he could go down to the airport and have a chat with the Sheikh while the plane was on the tarmac. In fact there was a reasonably senior Arabist in the embassy and so he had gone down and talked to Rashid. He vehemently denied having done or said anything which could have reinforced Rashid's delusions about British rule in Italy!

As already mentioned, despite the successful conclusion of the Jebel Akhdar operation which finally put an end to armed rebel activity in the form of ground actually held by rebel troops, there remained a good deal of sympathy for the rebel cause and the three leaders, Ghalib, Talib his brother and Suleiman bin Himyar, from their refuge in Saudi Arabia, conducted a clandestine campaign of sabotage against the Sultan of Oman and his supporters, the British. This took the form of mining the main roads and tracks, which was easy to do because none of the roads were tarmac, all being sand or gravel roads and tracks under which a mine could easily be concealed. The problem for the rebels was the getting of the mines into Oman from Saudi Arabia. There was no way of doing this and escaping detection except by camel because vehicles would be easily detected by the TOS or the SAF. Convoys of a few camels were numerous everywhere and, although sometimes mines were found when these were stopped and searched, it was impossible to deal with them all. So vehicles were continuously being blown up on tracks throughout Oman.

One of the methods resorted to by the rebels to avoid detection when smuggling mines into Oman was to bring them by dhow to the rugged fiords in the Musandam peninsula at the northern end of the range of mountains running north west from the Jebel Akhdar. There were no roads in the Musandam, only narrow and difficult mountain tracks, and the usual way north from Ras al Khaimah, the northernmost of the Trucial States, was by sea. The Musandam is a rugged series of peaks of up to 6,000 ft from which cliffs plunge straight down into the water. It gives the impression of being a long narrow mountain which has gradually sunk into the sea. Along the western side of this mountain is a series of narrow fiords at right angles to the coast, one of which leads through the mountain to the eastern side and one of which ends in a sheer cliff at least 1,000 ft high. Others afford shelter to dhows and from them tracks lead up into the mountain. The TOS dhow was used to patrol these inlets and to search any dhow found there for smuggled mines, but this was not an easy task and we supplemented the dhow patrols by reconnaissance from the air when a suitable aircraft was available.

On one of the occasions when I was doing the IO's job as well as my own in Sharjah, information came through that a dhow was about to unload a cargo of mines somewhere in the Musandam, and a Twin Pioneer aircraft was ordered to do a reconnaissance flight over the area to locate the dhow if it could be found, so that the Scouts dhow could deal with it. I went to the airfield armed with a map and binoculars to join the pilot who was a young Australian. He put me into the co-pilot's seat and we took off and set a course up the coast to the north east. He flew the aircraft and I spent my time searching the coast through the binoculars. After Ras al Khaimah we looked into one or two of the fiords to our right and saw nothing, and after a bit I said that soon we would reach the inlet that went through the Musandam to the east and if we took that we could cover the other side of the peninsula before returning to Sharjah. I suggested that we should circle for a few minutes over the sea while I made certain from the map which fiord was which. At this the pilot said that he was sure that the next inlet was the one through which we could fly to the other side because he recognised its entrance from the last time he had flown up to the Musandam and before I could remonstrate he had turned into the next inlet.

We were then about 5-600 ft above the water, flying into the mountain with vertical cliffs on either side which rose up at least another 500 ft. In front of us was a bend in the fiord and I fervently hoped that, as we turned it, we would have a view out over the sea the other side of the mountains. But to my horror, as we turned the bend we were confronted by a sheer cliff face which entirely shut off the end of the fiord. We were flying

A landlocked village on the eastern side of the Musandam

A village at the northern extremity of Ras al Khaimah, 1960

towards this cliff face with obviously no possibility of climbing up over it. I thought our last hour had come and was scared stiff. But the pilot was seemingly quite unperturbed and calmly pulled the wing flaps down to their fullest extent and slowly banked round with the aircraft's wheels, very nearly touching the cliff, until we were facing the way we had come and I breathed a great sigh of relief.

The Twin Pioneer was a fantastic aircraft as was its single engined version. It could virtually stop in mid air if necessary, as this experience showed, and of course the pilot knew its capabilities and therefore was not in the least perturbed by the incident. I knew it had a very short take off and landing capability, but had not realised how this could be used when faced with a cliff!

During my time with the Scouts the ruler of Sharjah was Sheikh Saqr bin Sultan al Qassimi whom I usually visited in his palace in the town, but one day he invited me to visit him in his date gardens in the foothills. This area was Sharjah territory, but separated from the town and its surroundings by the territory of another sheikhdom. This was a common feature of the seven sheikhdoms whose territories were in many cases separated from their main towns so that a map of the area with these territories in different colours resembled a patchwork quilt. Travelling round the area one often did not know whose territory one was in as there were no markings on the various boundaries. The Sharjah date gardens were in a beautifully fertile area of the foothills and when I arrived there I found that Sheikh Saqr had had groups of all his date varieties laid out on a sheet on the ground. He proudly told me that his gardens included over a hundred different sorts of date palms and invited me to try the various sorts and tell him which I liked best. I noticed that he was eating some small thin dates about the size of one's little finger or smaller and I tried some of those, but found them rather hard and bitter. Nearby I saw some large dates which looked sweet and delicious and I tried some of those. I found them incomparably better than the thin hard ones and said so. At that the sheikh laughed and said, "I thought you would probably like those best. In fact we feed them to the donkeys!"

For part of my tour with the Scouts I was in charge of the stables. Stewart Carter had managed to have ten chargers added to the establishment and had sent an officer up to Basra to buy these horses. One of them turned out to have belonged to Nuri Said, one time prime minister in Baghdad before the Ba'athist coup in 1958 in which he was killed. It was the best schooled of the horses and was later used by the Commander TOS on ceremonial parades. There was one fine black horse with a hard mouth which was difficult to control and I gave instructions that he was not to be ridden except by one of a short list of those I considered competent enough to control him. One day in the heat of summer an officer demanded to ride this horse and overrode the protests of the British sergeant in charge and rode out along the coastal track. The inevitable happened and he lost control and the horse ran away with him. The rider then decided to take the horse into the soft sand dunes in order to slow him down. In this he succeeded but only by dint of utterly exhausting the animal in a heat of about 120 degrees in the shade. I was called up to the stables late that evening to find the horse in his stable lying on the ground wrapped in a blanket and sweating profusely. I had the blanket removed and asked the sergeant why he had used it in an obvious case of heat stroke. The answer was that he had looked up 'exhaustion' in the book 'Animal Management in the Field' in which a blanket was recommended, but hadn't realised that the instruction referred to exhaustion in a temperate climate, not in the summer heat of the Gulf. I had not had experience of a horse with heat exhaustion before, but I knew what to do with a man with heat exhaustion, having suffered it myself, and decided to apply the same treatment to the horse.

So we spent the rest of the night applying cool water to the horse's body, hoping that he would recover, but it was not to be. As dawn broke he staggered to his feet and stood unsteadily for a short time leading us to think that he was recovering, but after two or three minutes fell dead to the ground.

That was very sad and raised the immediate problem of what to with the carcase. Regulations laid down that a horse should be buried in a pit of very considerable size, but it would be an enormous labour to dig such a pit in soft sand, so I ordered the sergeant to have the carcase taken down to the sea by the mouth of the creek and towed into deeper water where I was sure that the sharks which were common there would make short work of disposing of it. This was done and I breathed a sigh of relief. I then had to concoct a satisfactory account of what had happened in order to tell the chief veterinary officer who was due to visit us the next day from the headquarters in Aden that all the relevant regulations had been fully complied with.

This officer duly arrived the next day and he came into the mess for dinner. The Scouts officers' mess was still in an old coral and rock building on edge of the creek which ran parallel to the seashore for about a mile before ending in a tidal lake inland. It was like a tidal river, several feet deep and about fifty yards wide. The creek with its long dry sand bank and then the sea made a very pleasant view from the verandah at the end of the building where drinks were served before dinner. I sat down with the vet and gave him a drink and my assurances that we had dealt properly with the carcase seemed to be going down satisfactorily, when suddenly I saw what appeared to be four vertical black posts sticking out of the water in the distance near the mouth of the creek and slowly approaching on the tide. After a minute or two I realised with horror that it was the carcase of the dead horse which obviously had not been disposed of by the sharks. Luckily the vet had his back to the creek and the sea. There was only one thing to do and for the next fifteen minutes I kept him in animated conversation desperately hoping he would not turn round and see what was passing us on the tide. I breathed a sigh of relief when I saw the apparition disappear into the distance and I was able to stand up safely and take him in to dinner.

I thought that was the end of the problem, but after dinner I misjudged the state of the tide and before darkness fell I saw the four black sticks coming back down the creek when I was about to get the vet a coffee and

The Sharjah creek near the Scouts officers' mess, 1960

The mouth of Sharjah creek and the main track to Ajman, 1960

The Scouts officers' mess verandah overlooking the Sharjah creek and the open sea

a glass of port. Fortunately I was able to seat him again with his back to the creek and succeeded in keeping his attention for the second time until the carcase was out of sight beyond the point where the creek flowed out into the sea.

Another incident in the stables was unpleasant and not at all funny. It concerned the syces employed to look after the horses. The head syce was a charming elderly Pakistani called Buddha and the others, normally numbering four or five, were local Sharjah Arabs who were jealous of Buddha and wanted to get rid of him. Their leader came to me one day and said that Buddha had been behaving very badly and when I asked for details of his accusation he said that he had found Buddha late at night seriously maltreating one of the horses and that he should be sent home to Pakistan. When I asked him to elaborate on the details of the accusation he became evasive and merely repeated what he had said, but more forcefully and with more and more extravagant and unpleasant accusations.

When I mentioned this to Colonel Stewart Carter he said that the matter should be properly investigated and suggested an informal court of inquiry to look into the matter for Buddha's sake. So I organised that and

Buddha. The head syce (groom) at the Scouts' stables, 1960

had the syces all in to see what they had to say. Their leader made a series of unpleasant allegations, which were vehemently denied by Buddha and when I asked the other syces for their evidence on the matter they got themselves tied in knots and mutual contradictions. When I asked which of the horses Buddha had maltreated, the answer was that it had been the little bay mare and that he had banged an empty jerrican on the concrete floor of the stables behind her and hit her with a broomstick when she would not keep still as he groomed her tail. The thought of the little bay mare, the most nervous and sensitive horse in the stable, putting up with that treatment without kicking out in a fury was quite ridiculous and I and the other officers present had no difficulty at all in deciding that it was all a pack of lies. So I sacked the syce who had made the accusations, told the others what I thought of them for accepting the accusations and sent them away. Thereafter Buddha had no further trouble, but it had been an unpleasant episode.

The creek was the scene of another amusing incident during my time with the Scouts. The mess building was only a few feet from the waters of the creek and we seldom used the main ground floor door which was on that side of the building. It was in fact used for storage and in particular for storing the two sailing catamarans owned by the mess.

The Royal Navy which always had a frigate in the Gulf did not necessarily realise this and the frigates which visited us as a matter of routine were on detachment from the fleet in the Indian ocean. On one occasion when a frigate was about to visit us there was the usual exchange of signals and of invitations to dinner in the officers' mess and the sergeants' mess and I set up the usual arrangement for meeting the naval party when they disembarked and bringing them in to their destinations. They could not land opposite the officers' mess because they would then be confronted by the creek which was not visible from out at sea. So I said that I would have Land Rovers waiting by the old watch tower just beyond the creek entrance with their headlights shining out to sea at the appointed time before dinner.

This was duly done and we awaited the arrival of the Royal Navy. Some time elapsed and we were beginning to wonder what had happened. The lights of the ship were clearly visible offshore but we had no guests. Then suddenly there was a hammering noise from below the anteroom of the mess and we went downstairs to investigate. The noise was coming from the main door connecting the boathouse to the shore and when we opened it we were confronted by our naval guests in their mess dress, but stripped

A dinner party at the Scouts' HQ officers' mess, 1960

to their underpants from the waist down and with their nether garments held rolled up on top of their heads! They said they had seen the mess building and had headed straight for it and had disembarked and sent their boats back to the ship before they realised that after climbing up the beach they were confronted by what amounted to a none too clean river. Luckily the tide was low so no swimming was necessary as the water was only waist deep. After their tidying up and borrowing some shoes and socks we had a most enjoyable dinner. No one knew what had happened to the signal about the Land Rovers waiting at the old watch tower.

On one of these visits by the Navy the preliminary exchange of signals led to an amusing incident. The signals were sent by morse code and the Scouts boys' squadron were trained in morse. They knew no English but they were trained so that when they heard 'dot-dot-dot' they would write an English capital S on the message pad and that 'dash-dash-dash' meant that they must write O and so on. Perfectly intelligible messages could be quickly passed by this means and some of the boys of 12 or so became very good indeed. I'm told that in the signals world various small groups of letters are used to convey some comparatively complicated messages, such as SOS for instance, and there are several of these, amongst them a three letter group meaning, 'Your morse keying is unintelligible. Put on a more competent operator.'

On this occasion one of the Scouts boy signallers was on duty talking to the approaching frigate and found he could not understand the morse that was coming in from the ship, so he used this rather rude three letter group, hoping that he would be able to understand the morse from a different operator better. This indeed was the case and the exchange of signals went on as usual and the frigate anchored off shore. That evening when the naval party arrived at the Scouts sergeants' mess a burly very senior looking naval yeoman of signals demanded to talk to the Scouts sergeant in charge of the signals squadron, and then demanded to have the signaller in who had sent the rude message, because he, the yeoman of signals and the senior signals NCO on the frigate, had actually been manning the set himself at the time and wanted to tell the man concerned what he thought of him. The Scouts signals sergeant hid a grin and said he would go and get the man concerned. A few minutes later he returned with a diminutive 12 year old Arab boy whom he led up to confront the yeoman of signals who at first thought he was having his leg pulled, but then realised how the Scouts signals were organised and burst out laughing, patted the boy on the back and congratulated him on his expertise with the morse key.

CHAPTER 6

British Embassy Amman –
Kuwait Liaison Team

At the end of my tour with the Scouts Colonel Bartholomew took over as Commander TOS from Colonel Stewart Carter and I went home to 18 Field Regiment RA on Salisbury plain. I had been told that it was vital at that stage in my service that I should get up to date with the current tactics and equipment in the Regiment. In fact I found that the equipment, the 25 pounder gun, and its gun drill was exactly the same as it had been when I had first joined up during the war nearly twenty years before. Apart from that the equipment and organisation of a field regiment was less satisfactory than it had been. The guns were towed by 3 ton trucks instead of tractors and the batteries had been reduced from eight guns in two troops to six guns only, which was a far less flexible arrangement tactically. It did amuse me, after being told that I had been away from regimental service too long and that I needed to get up to date, to find that the field battery was a less effective unit than it had been and that its gun, the 25 pounder, was the gun I had trained on before I was commissioned in 1945. However I did an enjoyable stint of two years as a battery commander in the UK and Germany and was then posted out to the Arab world again as a junior military attache in Amman.

This was a very pleasant job because close military ties remained between the Jordanian and the British Armies and both were still organised on exactly the same lines with many of the Jordanian officers having done training courses in the UK. At that time, of course, Jordan still included what is now known as the West Bank and also the old city of Jerusalem, both later seized by the Israelis, and this fact made the territory much more interesting from the point of view of military intelligence than it later became after 1967. Jordan contained thousands of Palestinian refugees from the seizure of their land and property by the Jews in 1948. Many were still living in squalid camps near Amman with the more professional classes living in houses in Amman. All had lost houses and land in Palestine without any compensation and, meeting these people socially on a daily basis, my sympathies were entirely with them, particularly because their predicament was historically down to us, the British, for allowing unrestricted Jewish immigration when Palestine was under our Mandate.

In fact it is a little unfair to talk of unrestricted Jewish immigration at that time. We had in fact made efforts to control it, but it was a flood of immigration by sea which was very difficult to control. The British airborne gunner regiment which had been our neighbour in Quetta when I was in the Indian gunner regiment there, had been posted to Palestine at the time of Partition in India, and my friends in that regiment later told me what a difficult time they had had endeavouring to prevent Jewish immigrants disembarking at Haifa from the grossly overcrowded ships that were bringing them into the area from Europe. In one dreadful incident one of those ships was forced out to sea again after arrival off the coast of Palestine and it was so overloaded that it turned turtle and sank with great loss of life. Britain at that time was exhausted by years of war, both financially and as regards the morale of the Army, which was still manned largely by conscripts whose main desire in life was to return to 'civvy street' as soon as they could. Another factor was that the Jewish terrorist gangs operating in Palestine at that time made life most difficult and unpleasant, not only for the Palestinians but also for the British, as was shown when they blew up the King David Hotel, which housed a British Army HQ, and killed a large number of British Army people. So Palestine was by then a seemingly impossible problem which the British government was only too glad to hand over to the UN. It should be remembered, with all the current talk of Arab terrorism and how 'unacceptable' it is, that it was the Jews who first brought terrorism to the Middle East in modern times. A prime example of this was the massacre at Deir Yassin in 1948 of the Palestinian population numbering 250 men, women and children by a terrorist Jewish gang with the intention of terrifying the Palestinians of the whole area into fleeing from their villages. This was a successful ploy and thousands fled eastwards never to be able to return to this day to their houses and land.

The events leading up to the creation of the state of Israel are very largely forgotten by the world these days and it is generally regarded as a civilised country with all the consequent rights and duties of an established nation, but in Arab eyes it remains an illegitimate and aggressive American colony in the heart of the Arab world and the source of most of the many problems of the area during the last sixty years. This is particularly so in Jordan with its large population of dispossessed Palestinians and, in my time in that country, it was a topic of conversation which almost invariably arose when Palestinians and British found themselves together on social occasions.

One evening at a reception I remember meeting two Palestinian girls who had spent their childhood in Jerusalem before 1948. They told me that they had recently gone to Jerusalem in order to find the houses in which they had grown up and to meet the people now living in them. What they told me epitomised two extremes of the situation as regards the relationship between the Palestinians and the Jews of Israel. They found the first house and a woman spoke through a lattice in the gate and asked them in for coffee. She said she was delighted to see them and said that she and her husband had often thought of the owners of the house for which they had never paid a penny either to buy it or to rent it and they had always felt bad about that fact. The girls and the Israeli woman parted company on a most friendly basis.

After that they went in search of the second girl's house which they duly found and then knocked on the door. A woman opened the small door fitted to the main door and asked them what they wanted and the second girl began to explain that her family used to live there and that she would like to meet whoever was living there now. At that the woman spat and, shouting, "Filthy Arabs, go to hell", slammed the wicket shut. So, somewhat crestfallen, the two girls had come back to their families in Amman convinced that a solution to the problem of the dispossessed Palestinians was a very long way from being achieved. That story has stayed with me for many years and comes to mind every time I read of the Israeli government claiming to be the only democracy in the Middle East and referring to their Jewish population as occupying their reclaimed ancestral land after an absence of 2,000 years, the claim being based on the fact that it had been given them by God many centuries before that. I find myself imagining the chaos that could be caused between nations over international boundaries if such a claim were recognised as valid under international law.

I counted myself lucky in being posted as a military attache in such a friendly country in which the ties between the army and the British Army were so close and of such long standing. I found myself involved in various aspects of training in the Jordanian Army, from lecturing occasionally at their staff college to helping to arrange for their officers to go on training courses in the UK and getting up to date material from British training establishments on which the Jordanian staff college and other training courses were based. The one time when to my knowledge the Jordanians refused to go along with the then current British organisational changes was when the Jordanian artillery refused to change from eight gun field batteries to six gun batteries, a refusal with which I heartily agreed, having explained to the Jordanian gunners that, far from being a well thought out change made for valid operational reasons, it was in fact an unfortunate compromise between lack of money in the UK defence budget and the strong desire in the Regiment to maintain on the active list as many old established batteries as possible. Many had histories going back to Waterloo in 1815 and beyond.

During my time in India and in the Scouts I had become very keen on deer stalking and I made enquiries in the Jordanian Army HQ in Amman as to what one could stalk locally in Jordan. A friend told me that there were ibex in the hills east of the Dead Sea and that he could put me in touch with a tribal sheikh in the area who would probably be glad to help. In those days there was no road along the eastern shore of the Dead Sea and the mountains sloped steeply down into the water, so the routes south from Amman to Aqaba on the sea coast were either the centuries old road which still led through the ribbon of cultivated land and villages on the western edge of the desert or the road which ran south out in the flat desert. Amman on the edge of the desert is at a height of three thousand feet above sea level and the Dead Sea lies over one thousand feet below sea level, so from Amman and the old road south there is a very considerable mountainous drop down to the water. I took a few days off and went down to see the sheikh I had been told of and he received me most affably and said he would gladly send his son, Ahmed, with me as a guide to the area were ibex were likely to be found. The sheikh's son was a very friendly young man and was very keen to act as guide and said he would bring two of his tribesmen with a donkey and a camel to carry our kit and bedding. So we spent the night in the village and set off down the track to the Dead Sea in the morning. I noticed that my guide had a slight limp and had a nasty scar on the top of his right foot. When I asked him about the scar he blushed slightly and said that two or three years before he had accidentally shot himself in the foot and that it had been quite some time before he had been able to walk again without pain, but that now he could walk easily again, albeit with a slight limp. This has proved to be a unique occasion and I have never again met anyone who has literally 'shot himself in the foot'!

With the approach of nightfall I began to think of somewhere to spend the night and we went past a bend in the track where a few yards to one side there was a pleasant looking cave and I suggested that we should spend the night there. At this Ahmed vehemently shook his head and said that no one using the track would dream of stopping at that cave and that there were very good reasons not to do so. He seemed not to want to talk about it, but when I pressed him he told me the reason. He said, "The reason why we all avoid that cave is that we use it for a very special purpose. As you know rabies exists here although it is not common and every now and again someone gets bitten by a dog. It is then the accepted practice that the person should be securely tied up in that cave and should be left with plenty of bread and water for a week. At the end of that time we go to the cave to see how the victim has fared. We either find the person dead, or alive and well and very pleased to see us again. So then we either have a funeral or a celebratory feast to mark the occasion. We accept the fact that no one can do anything to help someone with rabies and the nearest doctor is miles away. So we avoid any possibility of anyone else getting infected by doing what we consider best for everyone including the victim."

After this we continued down the hill track to the bottom of the valley where there was a stream and an inviting looking cave nearby. Ahmed said that this was the best place for us to spend the night and so we unloaded our kit and settled down round a fire which had been quickly lit with the sticks and small branches which were lying about on the hillside. The sheikh had told me not to worry about food because he had told Ahmed to make sure that he had provisions for three days for the whole party. So I asked Ahmed what was for supper and he replied, "Mohammed will make some mujallala." I wondered what that was, but I was soon to see. Mohammed produced a battered enamelled tin bowl and put a little water in it. Then he produced some flat wholemeal unleavened bread and put two round pieces into the water. One of the others handed him two hardened balls of dried yoghurt about the size of snooker balls which he broke into pieces with a stone. I noticed at this stage that his hands were none too clean, particularly his fingernails, and watched fascinated while he pushed back his shirt cuffs and began kneading the bread and the pieces of dried yoghurt into the water in the bowl. He continued to squash the mixture between his fingers until it turned into a paste of the consistency of milky porridge and then declared the dish ready and washed his hands in the stream. I saw that his hands and fingernails were now as clean as if he had scrubbed them with soap and water! I was handed some fresh dry bread and we all set to, Arab fashion, to tear off small pieces of bread, fashion them into a spoon shape in the right hand and dip them into the paste in the bowl. I was fairly hungry after the day's march and found this dish of 'mujallala' pleasantly filling and well flavoured when I had succeeded in banishing the thought of Mohammed's fingernails from my mind.

The next day we set off again down towards the Dead Sea valley and Ahmed said we were now approaching the area where we would probably find ibex, but, on breasting a ridge, we saw in the distance a shepherd with a herd of goats and sheep. Ahmed was aghast at the sight and said that the shepherd must have come over from the western side of the valley which was unprecedented in his experience, but that it did mean that any ibex in the area would have moved a long way away, probably to the south, and that we would need another three days at least to find any.

Unfortunately this was impossible if only because we had not brought enough food with us to extend the trip for so long and, in any case, I had to get back to Amman to catch up with my work. So, reluctantly, we turned back and wound our way up through the hills to Ahmed's village. There I stayed the night again before driving back to Amman. Despite the failure to find any ibex it had been a most enjoyable few days and I had made some new friends.

In due course my time in Amman came to an end and, after some home leave, I was posted on promotion to Kuwait to join the Kuwait Liaison Team. This was a small military mission whose job it was to train the Kuwait armed forces. My task was to train the army staff in military intelligence, which consists in manning the rearward communications of the HQ, gathering information on what an enemy force is doing 'the other side of the hill' and working out what he is capable of doing and what his future actions are likely to be. At least this was the job I expected to find myself doing, but when General Mubarak, the army commander, came back from a long period of leave in the summer he told me he wanted me to set up and train what amounted to a combination of MI5 and MI6 in addition to the task in the army HQ which I had assumed was the object of my posting. When I pointed out that there was in Kuwait a retired British colonial police officer doing exactly that job for the Kuwait Ministry of the Interior and said that I thought it was unnecessary to set up such an organisation within the Army HQ as well, he replied, "Surely, colonel, you have enough experience of the Arab world to realise that an army headquarters needs such an organisation precisely because there is one in the Ministry of the Interior and we in this headquarters need to know what they are up to as well as knowing about the hostile activities of other states." I was taken aback by this, but made no further comment at the time and later told the Ambassador that I felt that I should return to the UK on the grounds that there had obviously been a misunderstanding and that I had not got the expertise that the general assumed I had. The Ambassador's reaction was that he did not like the idea of my leaving at all and said that he thought that the Kuwaitis would be upset if I told the general that I wanted to leave. He told me that there were other problems that were making our relationship with the Kuwaitis a little tricky at the time and he asked me to stay on and make the best of the situation. He suggested that I should go and have a talk with the retired British colonial policeman who was attached to the Ministry of the Interior in an advisory and training role and see if he had any useful suggestions.

So that evening I went round to see the retired police officer, John Brown, and explained the problem. It turned out that he had been the head of the special branch of the police in West Africa covering Nigeria and the Gold Coast (now Ghana). He told me that he had written a training manual on the duties and methods of the special branch which were essentially the same as those of MI5. He would let me have a copy and I could base my work on it and come and have a chat with him at any time if I had difficulties. So I gratefully accepted that solution and asked him if he had any ideas as regards MI6. He said, "As a matter of fact I have. My job in West Africa did not cover the sort of activities covered by MI6, but I do have a copy of the papers produced by the Russian defector who came over to the West a couple of years ago. As you know, the activities carried out overseas by MI6 are covered in the Soviet Union by their army through their military attaches, and this senior Russian defector, to prove his bona fides, handed over the complete training manual used at the Soviet military attache training school. This was translated by us into English and I have a copy here which you can have." This answered all my problems. Of the three subjects I needed to teach the first was conventional intelligence staff work as taught at the Staff College, the second, the MI5 aspect, was covered by John Brown's manual and the fact that he was available for expert advice, and the third was covered by the Soviet attache training manual. I had no idea by how much that differed from the MI6 equivalent, but the chances that I could be given a copy of the latter were nil. So I felt well pleased and set about constructing a course of training covering the whole field and translating it all into Arabic. I thus found myself with a full time job which I found fairly stimulating, although it was marred by the fact that I had nothing to do with the choice of my students most of whom turned out to be less than suitable for the task.

John Brown warned me that I would probably encounter problems and cited one of his own. In his training programme he had often emphasized the importance of the utmost confidentiality and discretion in the business of choosing, controlling and paying agents. Some time later when he thought he had a well organised and well trained department in the ministry he had come to his office and had had to pass a long queue of people waiting in the street outside the main door of the building. So he had asked his people what the queue was about. "Oh", they said,"Those are all the agents you told us to recruit. Today is their pay day"!

The senior member of the four officers of lieutenant colonel or equivalent rank in the KLT was Robin Wright and it was he and his wife Trish who made life in Kuwait enjoyable for me where otherwise I think I would have asked for another posting after a year or so. I also had some good friends amongst the Kuwaitis. The other people who made my life enjoyable were the Ambassador, Geoffrey Arthur, and his Counsellor, John Graham, who were very conscious of the problems of service in the KLT and did a great deal to ensure that we were always made welcome in the Embassy community.

One of the episodes which took place in the Gulf during my time in Kuwait was the abrupt announcement from the Labour government in London in early 1968 that it had been decided that Britain would end its treaties of protection with the Gulf states and withdraw all its remaining forces from the area by the end of 1971. What was so appalling about this precipitate decision was the manner of its development. Some months before, a junior minister in Harold Wilson's Government had been deputed to visit the Rulers of the Gulf states to sound out their opinions on the continued presence of British power and influence in the Gulf. This had developed over a period of nearly three centuries and in 1968 Britain was the accepted protecting power with treaty responsibilities for the defence and foreign relations of all the Arab Gulf states, with the exception of Saudi Arabia. It was thought that this situation could not go on for ever and that the Rulers concerned should be consulted on the matter. I remember meeting this minister at a reception at the Embassy. His name was Goronwy Roberts and he seemed to be a most sensible and unbiased man. He went on his way round the Gulf meeting all the Rulers and asking them for their opinions. We soon heard that they had been unanimous in their opinion that things should remain as they were. They preferred it that the British should remain responsible for the defence and good order in the Gulf. None wanted to take on the responsibility and costs of doing it for themselves. The minister had given assurances to them all that Britain would maintain the status quo for the foreseeable future until the Rulers decided otherwise.

We were dumbfounded when, only a few weeks later, the same man toured the Gulf and told all the Rulers that the British Government had changed its policy and had decided it would withdraw its forces and unilaterally shed its treaty responsibilities in the Gulf by the end of 1971. This decision did immense damage to the reputation of the British in the area. The Rulers considered it a very public slap in the face and were angry that such an important change of policy should apparently have been taken without any further consultation. Indeed, the Rulers of Abu Dhabi and Dubai offered privately to contribute money for the cost of maintaining British forces in the Gulf if lack of finance was the reason for the decision. This was refused and the Prime Minister went so far as to make a public statement on the offer and his refusal of it, which did nothing to improve British relations with the Gulf States

It was later reported that this fiasco was due to a sudden financial crisis and a debate in cabinet at which Barbara Castle, confronted by a demand to reduce certain proposed expenditure in the Health Service, demanded that the cut should come out of the defence budget, pointing out that the cost of Britain's defence responsibilities in the Gulf nicely covered the sum her Health Service budget needed. Whatever the causes, it was a sad and shaming day for Britain, in her decline from the status of a world power of long standing, to allow it to be published abroad that important decisions of foreign policy were now taken in such a fickle and inconsequential way.

CHAPTER 7

Defence Attache – Lebanon and Syria

At the end of my tour in the Kuwait Liaison Team I was told I would be posted as Defence Attache Lebanon. I said that, in my experience in the area, DA Beirut as a job was a bit of a waste of time and that I did not want to do it. I would take an attache job but not there. The people in the Ministry of Defence then said that I would be DA Syria as well as Lebanon as soon as diplomatic relations were restored and that seemed imminent. I would then move to Damascus. So on that basis I accepted Beirut and moved there to take up the post.

As things turned out, I did a stint of three years in the job in Beirut and never moved to Damascus. This was because every time it looked as if diplomatic relations were about to be restored some international event involving Britain took place which offended the Syrian government and negotiations were broken off. However, I did remain responsible for Syria as regards reporting to the Ministry of Defence in London and I travelled in Syria extensively and often called on the Ministry of Defence in Damascus. So I did not miss much and still had plenty to do. The one thing I did miss was promotion!

British policy towards Syria was, I thought, misguided. Because of the powerful Jewish lobby in the USA, the Americans have evolved a policy of staunch and unwavering support for Israel and for whatever its government decides to do. Add to this the fact that British policy aligns itself closely with that of the USA and one sees why Britain adopts a hostile attitude to Syria as a potential military threat to Israel. It was this attitude and the refusal by Britain to supply military equipment to Syria that drove the Syrians into the arms of the Russians at the time of the 'Cold War' and this situation lasted for a long time. It was as if the House of Commons had to have a 'whipping boy' in its consideration of policy towards the Middle East and had chosen Syria for this role. I have found that Syrian people as a whole have friendly feelings towards the British on a personal level. In my job in Beirut I was free to travel throughout Syria merely by turning up at the border and saying who I was. The Syrians were all most friendly, although they did keep an eye on my movements. On one occasion I took a party from the Beirut Embassy to Palmyra, the ancient ruined city in the middle of the Syrian desert, and on leaving that place decided to head straight north east across the desert away from all the roads and tracks to Dura Europos, another ancient ruin on the banks of the Euphrates river. We camped for the night halfway across the desert and the next day saw a helicopter circling the desert in the distance. When it came to where we were it circled over us twice and flew away. The Syrians had obviously wondered where on earth we had got to.

A few years later, when I was living in Jordan, there was some political row between Syria and London and for a time no British were allowed into Syria. I wanted to drive back to the UK from Jordan and would have to cross Syria first, so I had to bide my time until the travel ban was lifted and I could set out. At the border post on the road to Damascus I went into the Syrian immigration office and proffered my passport saying, "I thought you Syrians did not like the British, but it's nice to be here again." At that the man behind the desk said with a broad grin, "We're very fond of the British, but we do hate Margaret Thatcher! Welcome to Syria".

While I had freedom to travel in Syria a good BBC friend of mine, Eric Bowman, who was living in Beirut and who knew I travelled quite often round Syria, asked me when I was talking to people in the villages to find out from them what they thought of the BBC and what reception was like. So, when I was chatting to people about what was going on in the world, I used to ask where they got their news from. "Damascus?, The Voice of America?", I used to ask. Almost always the answer was, "No we don't trust either of those. They tell a lot of lies, but we know we always get the truth from the BBC". Eric was very gratified when I told him that. I often used to wonder how strictly the output of the Arab announcers on the BBC Arabic Service was monitored.

One of my colleagues amongst the military attaches in Beirut was the Russian MA with whom I got on particularly well. I thought him a very nice and competent man and, since I had been warned about how to avoid the risk of being suborned by him as several British had been in the past by other Russian attaches around the world, I wondered whether he would eventually try the technique on me. Sure enough he invited me round for a drink or coffee at his place and I reciprocated until one day he asked me if I could get him a map of London and its surroundings. This was the first and absolutely innocuous step in the ploy that I had been warned about, so I said, "Well, I don't have any maps here, but the simplest thing for you to do is to write to your MA in London and ask him to go out to a good bookshop and buy a map for you. It's the simplest thing in the world to buy any sort of map of England you like in London. Why don't you do that?" So he smiled a knowing smile as if to say, 'I'm not going to get anywhere with you with that gambit, but it was my duty to try it and now I can report that I have done so'. After that we continued to get on extremely well. We had been told in London that the technique was to ask initially for quite innocuous favours which gradually became less and less innocent until, in the end, one found oneself providing secret papers, and one was securely hooked by threats of exposure.

At one stage in my time in Beirut I was told by the MoD to go over to Damascus to the Syrian Army HQ to ask them if they wanted to buy any British military equipment. I replied that, in the light of our then political relationship with Syria, it would be more sensible if I went with a list of what equipment we were willing to supply to them. The answer to that was that my suggestion was unnecessary and would I kindly go and do what had been asked of me. So I went to Damascus and went to see the general in charge of equipping the army and asked him what he would like to buy from Britain. Predictably he replied that he thought it would save a lot of unnecessary work if I could tell him what could be allowed to be supplied to Syria. He suspected that it would not be very much. I said that I had asked for such a list on the grounds that it would save possible embarrassment, but that I had been told just to do what had been asked. So he said, "I'll write you a quick list" and took a pencil and a piece of paper and wrote a list and handed it to me. At the top he had written '50 medium tanks' and then various numbers of armoured cars, guns, machine-guns, cargo trucks, ambulances and sundry medical supplies including a large supply of bandages. He handed the list to me saying,"These are what I would like, but I'm willing to bet that your government will sell us none of those things except the ambulances." So I thanked him and left, saying that I would return with an answer.

I sent the list to London and, sure enough, when the answer came back some days later the tanks were refused, but so were all the other main items including the ambulances. When I asked why we had even refused those the answer was that they had decided that the ambulances could too easily have a heavy machine gun mounted on them and be transformed into offensive troop carrying vehicles. I suspect that the Israeli authorities may have been consulted about the list and had crossed out everything except the bandages. I was then faced with the embarrassing prospect of going over to see the Syrian general again to tell him that he had won his bet. When I saw him about it he was most pleasant to me and we parted on good terms.

My relationship with the Lebanese Army was both friendly and cordial. It was a small army but most of the officers were well trained and well qualified, many having attended courses in the UK, France or America. I was also impressed by the soldiers I met. I made it a habit to give a lift to any soldier I saw on the road as I was driving round the country and, while being careful not to ask any questions about their units, I always asked what their religion was and what part of the population of the country they came from. The answer invariably was that religion played no part in the Lebanese Army and was never mentioned or discussed. I found this most impressive, as it showed that it was a well enforced policy to keep religious and sectarian differences out of the army. The emphasis was on the fact that everyone was Lebanese wherever they came from and whatever their origin. This was wholly admirable in a country with such wide and numerous sectarian differences as there were in Lebanon. The population was roughly half Christian and half Muslim, with a substantial proportion being Druze, an offshoot of Shiite Islam. Then about half the Muslims are Shiite and half Sunni. The Christians are mostly Maronite but other sects are well represented. This has always been the cause of strife and bloodshed in the past and the army was intent on preventing any future religious problems. This feeling was widespread amongst the younger part of the population. Young people entering universities, when confronted by an initial questionnaire form, were in the habit of putting a line through the box which asked for details of their religion. Marriages between Christians and Muslims were no longer unheard of.

Unfortunately this policy began to fail in my time and the reason was mainly due to the influx of a large number of refugees from Palestine in 1948 when the Jews seized a large part of that country. The Lebanese government had received the refugees amicably, as had the other neighbouring states, but had expected the West and the UN to intervene before long and secure the return of the refugees to their land. They therefore did not plan for a long term presence of those people in their country and allowed them to set up extensive camps in the sparsely populated area between Beirut city and the main airport some miles to the south on the coast. As the Palestinian population remained from year to year tents gave way to buildings and apathy changed to militancy so that the Palestinians became a serious political and military threat to the state, a threat made more acute by the strategic position of the camps which allowed the Palestine Liberation Organisation to cut the city off from its airport whenever they wished. In my time in Beirut the PLO began to amass weapons in the camps and to create their own small army. The Lebanese Army and police agreed not to enter the area and to leave the maintenance of law and order to the PLO which went from strength to strength in the camps, until it became a threat to the very existence of the state. It was then decided that the armed forces must intervene and I remember watching the Lebanese Air Force squadron of Hunter fighter bombers strafing the camps with bombs and rocket fire. After that there was a truce and things appeared to return to normal, but damage to the structure of Lebanese society had been done. Not only was there the large refugee camp just south of Beirut, but there was another such camp, albeit smaller, adjacent to the northern city of Tripoli. Tensions between the Muslim and the Christian sections of the population began to appear. Some families which had branches of both religions existing amicably side by side began to split on religious lines, a thing that people had believed had become impossible. By the time I left Beirut shooting incidents between rival groups were becoming more and more common and the country slowly slid into a state of civil war which was to last for several years.

So my tour of duty in Beirut ended on a sad note after three years and I was faced with a decision over my future, either to stay on in the Army doing mundane jobs at home, or to retire from the service and find another job elsewhere for the next few years. At this stage it had become obvious that my marriage to my wife Mary was no longer working well. Unfortunately the many years that I had spent working abroad, sometimes with her and sometimes leaving her at home, had put a great strain on our marriage. She had finally got very tired of diplomatic life in Beirut and had gone home some time before my tour there ended. So we regretfully decided to part company.

CHAPTER 8

The Defence Industry

Towards the end of my time as defence attaché in Beirut, covering Lebanon and Syria, it was suggested to me by the then Adjutant General, General Wilson, that I should go to Oman to be chief of staff to General Ken Perkins, the commander of the Sultan's Armed Forces. General Wilson had been my instructor at the Staff College and so it was good to see him again when he came out on a visit to Beirut. He said that I had missed my chance of promotion to colonel because I had done too many wrong things in my career, two years at Cambridge reading law, nearly two years learning Arabic at MECAS, and two years with the Trucial Oman Scouts. There was a long list of officers who had done all the right things and only so many vacancies for promotion. He suggested that if I went to Oman I would get temporary promotion to colonel and then, at regular retirement age, could stay on as a contract officer until I finally retired. Furthermore Ken Perkins, CSAF, was also a gunner.

This was most tempting, but several of my friends advised that, if I joined a British company before I was 51, I would get on to their pension scheme and then probably continue in the company until I reached 65, long after I would have had to retire from SAF. This seemed to me to be the most sensible course despite the attractions of going to Muscat, so I decided to retire from the Army when I left Beirut. I have often felt regrets at not having gone to Ken Perkins as his chief of staff, particularly as we later found ourselves working together in industry and became good friends. In those days he often referred to me as the officer who had refused to join his staff! He would add that the decision had proved right for me as things turned out.

When I finally left Beirut at the end of my time there I doubted whether I should find another job that was so rewarding and which gave me such freedom to travel virtually where and when I wanted. In fact a year later I was in a job that was just as interesting and which gave me even more freedom to go where and when I liked. As defence attaché I was basically confined to Lebanon and Syria, whereas in British Aerospace I was free to travel throughout the Arab world at any time. But that job was over a year away.

The Army treated me very well over my retirement. One alternative open to me was to continue to 55 as a 'special list' lieutenant colonel doing essentially a major's job on the staff somewhere. One continued on one's existing rate of pay and some of the jobs were reasonably attractive. However, knowledgeable friends, notably my old friend John Pattinson, who had been in Quetta when I was, told me that with my Middle East qualifications, the language and knowledge of so many countries in the area, I should be able to get a good job in industry, especially because of the rapidly increasing commercial importance of the Arab world at that time. And so it proved, and I was taken on by the British Aircraft Corporation as soon as I applied to them. I joined the Guided Weapons Division at Stevenage which manufactured the Rapier low level anti-aircraft missile system in service with the Army and the RAF. BAC was marketing this system in the Arab world and in Iran and was recruiting and training people to provide training teams in customer countries when sales were achieved. So I found myself doing a training course on Rapier, which was interesting and enjoyable, and also taking part in marketing meetings. This went on for several months and I learnt many new things about industry. Much of it seemed inexplicable to me, but when I asked why something was being done in a way that seemed all wrong to me, I was told that people from the services were always asking questions of that sort, that it always took a considerable time for them to realize the wisdom of industrial methods and that I should bide my time and all would be revealed in due course. It was several weeks before I realized that there was in fact no secret to be learnt and that what seemed stupid to me as a man from the Army was indeed stupid, and often easily avoidable. In particular the marketing and commercial departments responsible for overseas sales consistently failed to match the high quality of the products they were attempting to sell.

For instance on a marketing trip to Abu Dhabi, with several people from the marketing staff and a couple from the commercial branch, I asked to see the text of the offer which was to be given to the commander of the Abu Dhabi Defence Force. The commercial man demurred and said that the commercial people never let the marketing men see such documents. After some argument eventually I was given sight of the offer which was for a complete battery of Rapier including four launchers, two radars, a dozen or so Land Rovers and a supply of missiles. The prices seemed high to me, but of course the development costs of the system had been high over the years and BACGW needed to make a decent profit. I had no idea what the prices for a Rapier launcher or the missiles should be, but I did think that many of the prices for the Land Rovers seemed excessive, although I realized that several of them would need to be considerably modified for the jobs they needed to do in the battery. However I did notice that half a dozen of these vehicles were listed as plain long wheelbase Land Rovers WD pattern, with no indication of any modifications by BAC, and yet the price quoted I knew to be much higher than the price charged by the vehicle maker in the UK. So I asked what modifications the company had done to those vehicles. The answer was that none at all had been done, but that the total price had been calculated on the basis of individual prices for the various items, and then, due to some changes in the field of finance, a further sum had had to be added and it had been decided by the commercial department that the increase should be spread as a percentage across all the items in the offer. I pointed out that, although no one could possibly gainsay a price quoted for a launcher or a missile, when it came to a simple unmodified Land Rover the customer had only to phone the local Land Rover agent to find that the price quoted was nearly double the price of the same vehicle available locally, and that this would not reflect well on the company. I said that to my mind, if these sums were added to the very much larger prices for the launchers or the missiles there could be no problem. The only answer I received was the familiar one. BAC always produced their offer figures that way and that when I had been longer with the company I would no doubt realise the wisdom of their methods.

Another good example of the haphazard workings in industry occurred a year or two later. Prior to my arrival on the scene there had been a strong marketing tussle in Abu Dhabi between us and the French after the Rulers had declared their intention to acquire a low level air defence capability. Their choice was either the French Crotale system or our equivalent, Rapier. The two systems were designed for the same low level air defence capability, but there was a fundamental difference between the two designs. Crotale had a much larger warhead than Rapier, but it had a proximity fuse which could do considerable damage to an aircraft even if it missed by several feet, whereas Rapier had a small warhead and had to hit the target to explode. The great advantage of the Rapier system lay in the fact that the launcher and the missile were much lighter than those of Crotale and this very much simplified the deployment and the logistics of the system.

In the event the Abu Dhabi staff decided to acquire a battery of each system together with a number of missiles in order to conduct their own trials. There was then a considerable delay while the details were thrashed out and the necessary aerial targets arranged. Then the trials were held. The Crotale system did fairly well, but the Rapier missiles which were fired went all over the place. Certainly none hit the target.

That effectively ended the chances of our selling Rapier in the Gulf for the foreseeable future. The company conducted an immediate enquiry and it transpired that it was known in the missile supply side of the company that the batch of missiles sold some time previously to Abu Dhabi were possibly defective because the gyroscope motors, essential for the accurate control of the missiles, might have been contaminated by damp during manufacture. This had been suspected by the manufacturing staff but they had decided to say nothing and hope for the best, even when they knew that a crucial public trial was in the offing. As far as I know no action was taken as regards those responsible despite the fact that their actions resulted in greatly reducing such chances as we had of selling Rapier elsewhere in the Gulf states.

Later a Rapier demonstration was held in the UK at a coastal anti-aircraft artillery range in an effort to repair the damage to the reputation of the Rapier system. It was said that the missiles in Abu Dhabi must have deteriorated locally in storage because the company's rules about temperature and humidity control had not been properly observed. So another demonstration was required to do the system justice.

There is no doubt that the Rapier Blindfire system is very accurate and effective. Once the radar has locked on to the target the missile is automatically controlled to follow the radar beam until it hits the target, but once again its reputation was undermined by marketing shortcomings. In this case the target was a radio controlled aircraft and all the potential customers for the system were invited to attend. No expense was spared and the Army gave its full support, supplying a Rapier fire unit and staff to give a technical commentary during the demonstration. The target aircraft duly appeared and flew past over the sea and a missile was launched at it, but there was no explosion and the aircraft flew on apparently unharmed. It was still under control and was brought back past the firing point and another missile was launched at it. This time there was a malfunction and the missile shot up almost vertically into the sky. The target flew on and disappeared. It was announced over lunch that an aircraft had been sent up to look at the target aircraft and had reported that it had been holed in the fuselage. The marketing director then explained that, due to the safety regulations at the range, the missiles had had to be fitted with inert warheads and that the direct hit had by an extraordinary fluke not resulted in any damage to the aircraft. He had relied on the belief that a hit even with an inert warhead would bring the target aircraft down. Had he explained at the start that the warheads were inert the spectators might have believed that the demonstration had been at least 50% successful. As it was, none of the spectators believed that and they all left for their London hotels, convinced that the demonstration had been a complete failure.

In fact control of the aircraft was regained when it was out of sight of the onlookers and it was successfully landed, whereupon it was discovered that one of the missiles had hit the cockpit and had made a neat hole through the fuselage without damaging any of the control systems. The spectators were told the facts back in London but the reaction was one of disbelief and the attitude was that it must have been very easy when the plane had been recovered for someone to take a crowbar and simulate the damage to the fuselage. So there was another failure and a most expensive one. Although it must be said that what had happened was partly due to bad luck the fact remains that, had the marketing director in charge of the trial briefed the viewers properly the damage done to the reputation of the Rapier system could have been much reduced.

I had only been with BAC for a few months when I was headhunted by the company on the other side of the road in Stevenage. This was the Space Division of Hawker Siddeley Dynamics which had decided to branch out from making military communications satellites into the commercial satellite field and wanted to recruit someone to live in the Arab world to do the necessary marketing, aiming for the new satellite for the Arab Satellite Organisation, later named 'Arabsat'. I learnt this when I went to see the man who first suggested that someone should be appointed to do this job. This was Bertie Wootten, Air Commodore retired, a well known ex service figure who had boxed for the RAF and flown in the Battle of Britain. He became my boss initially for the first part of my job in Amman which eventually extended to a period of over fourteen years. I arrived in his office and we discussed the details of the job.

It seemed to me to be a wonderful opportunity. I was told I could, within reason, live where I liked, and that I would have to do the marketing work in all the countries which were members of the Arabsat organization. That meant nearly all the Arab countries and certainly all the major ones. Previously the obvious place to live for someone doing a Middle East marketing job would have been Beirut where I had many friends after my time as defence attache there. Indeed while the job was first under discussion Beirut was assumed to be the base, but the civil war there was getting worse by the week until finally the embassy advised the British to avoid Lebanon. It was then obviously a silly idea to think of going there. One alternative was Cyprus and many of the people doing my sort of job went there. But I decided on Amman because I knew the place well and had friends there and because I regarded it as axiomatic that, for an Arab world marketing job, one must live in an Arab capital. Then, whenever one wanted to know what was going on in another Arab country, there would be someone nearby who would know the answer. That is not the case in Cyprus.

The managing director of the Space Division, Peter Hickman, while hurriedly leaving the office a day or two later, asked where I had decided to live and I said "Amman", at which he said, "Fine" and left. The next day he called me in and said, "Why do you want to go and live so far to the edge of your area?" I said, "Amman couldn't really be more in the centre of the area. What do you mean?" He took out his diary and turned to the map and pointed to Oman and said, "Look. That couldn't be further from the centre". I said, "I'm talking about Amman not Oman!" and I started to point it out to him on his map, but found that Amman was completely obliterated by a label overprinted on the map saying 'Charles Letts and Co'!

Initially, living in Amman doing my new job with Hawker Siddeley Dynamics Space Division, my task was to travel round the Arab countries which were members of the Arabsat board of directors, to talk to the ministers of communications and their staffs. I needed to tell them that HSD were now in the business of providing commercial communications satellites, based on their expertise in providing military satellites for the UK Ministry of Defence, and that we would now like to bid for the first Arabsat satellite. The invitation to tender for Arabsat 1 was due before long. This meant that my first priority was to visit the more important Arab states which were contributing the greater part of the finance for the project.

In most cases this involved paying a courtesy call on the minister of communications to talk about the company in general terms, and then visiting his technical staff, usually Egyptian, to talk in more detail. I had had a period of technical briefing at Stevenage by John Watson, a leading expert on the technology, so that I could talk sense about satellites with the technical people as well as could be expected for one with no degree in any science subject, although it helped that I had in the past done the first year's syllabus for the BSc physics course at Edinburgh. This programme went well and most of the conversations were conducted in English.

However, there were exceptions where it was necessary to talk Arabic on these visits. The composition of the Arabsat board was rather like that of the UN Security Council in that the most important Arab countries were permanent members, but at least two places were allotted periodically and in rotation to the minor member states where ministers were not necessarily familiar with English. I took care therefore to mug up on the Arabic words for the more technical terms required in a general briefing on the subject of communications satellites. For instance the Arabic term for satellite is 'artificial moon' and one had to have the necessary words to convey the meaning of 'geostationary orbit', meaning the orbit round the earth whose distance from the surface of the planet is such that the centrifugal and gravitational forces acting on a satellite are so balanced that the satellite remains stationary in relation to a point on the earth's surface.

When I visited Qatar on one occasion I had a very useful talk with the Egyptian technical people in the ministry, after which I asked to see the minister, at which the technical staff laughed and said that I would be wasting my time because he was merely a figurehead tribal sheikh who was related to the Ruler. I persisted on the principle that it was important to make friends with as many people as possible who were part of the Arabsat organisation. So I found myself talking about satellites to a charming and venerable bedouin sheikh who asked me how far up in the sky these satellites had to be. I then explained all about geostationary orbits in my best Arabic and he asked just how high this orbit was. I said that it was 22,000 miles above the earth. At this he turned and gazed out of the window at the view of the desert stretching away into the distance and there was a long pause, and then he said, "22,000 miles! That must need a very very long length of rope!"

I realised that my explanation of geostationary orbits had not been very effective, but in fact the visit proved later to have been thoroughly worthwhile because, thereafter, whenever I went to one Arab capital or another to be on hand for a meeting of the Arabsat board it was always the old Qatari sheikh who was the most effusive and friendly in his greeting and, indeed, he did tell me several very useful things about how the various meetings were going.

My initial period living in Amman and travelling round the Middle East was confined to marketing activity concerning Arabsat, but it was not long before I found myself marketing the other products of Hawker Siddeley, first the ground and air missile systems and then the aircraft such as Harrier and Hawk. And then again it was not long before the aircraft and missile producing parts of Hawker Siddeley were amalgamated with the British Aircraft Corporation to form British Aerospace and I found myself doing the Middle East marketing for all the products of both companies including the Rapier low level anti-aircraft missile system, which had been my introduction to industry on leaving the Army.

I had a most enjoyable time living in Amman working for BAe and the company always treated me very well. Early on in this period I had married again and my wife Celia gave birth to our son, Peter, in 1977. So for the best part of 14 years in Jordan we were living happily in Amman as a family. It was a constantly changing scene as regards the marketing of defence equipment. As soon as one opportunity arose somewhere I would go to the place concerned, visit all the people involved in the decision and advise the company how to proceed. Then if that came to nothing there was always another project somewhere else before long. One very frustrating aspect of working for BAe concerned the choice of agents. To sell anything of value in the Arab world one needs local advice and assistance and the choice of the right people to provide that help for a reasonable commission is essential. I considered that I, constantly travelling round the area, meeting the local entrepreneurs and the knowledgeable people in the British embassies and speaking the language, was obviously better placed than anyone back in the UK to choose the local helpers in each case. So I found it infuriating when, as happened several times, my advice was ignored, and help was sought in London from some Arab entrepreneur, probably living in Belgrave Square, and I was told that I need not even know the man's name. In fact it was not difficult to find the name out from local sources and it usually turned out to be someone who had had success in the past in the country concerned, but who to my mind was now useless because since then there had been a complete change amongst the local decision makers. This happened again and again and we lost a number of contracts.

A typical instance was when I had worked on a sale of a squadron of Hawk advanced training aircraft to the Jordanian Air Force and the project was nearly home and dry when I advised that someone senior should come out to Jordan and shake hands on a deal for our local man's commission. Part of the company's policy in these matters which I did in fact agree with was that someone resident abroad, as I was, should not take part in the actual meetings with the agent at which commission figures were agreed.

86

So one of the junior directors, David Hastie, came out and duly shook hands on an agreement with the local man I had chosen and then left saying that written confirmation would follow. Then there was apparently a change in the senior hierarchy in the company at home and the new sales director told me on the phone that he did not agree with what had occurred, and that he would pursue the project in his own way. I emphasised that a director of the company had shaken hands on an agreement and to my mind that was that. I was sure that the project would go through. All that was needed was confirmation in writing. But the new man merely said that he would not go through with it and that he would pursue the matter in another way. The result was that the project went to our competitors.

Over my period with the company every two or three years there was an invitation to tender for a new Arabsat satellite. This was because the life of a satellite in orbit was inevitably limited. On some of these occasions a stage arrived when success was very probable after a careful and lengthy marketing effort. Each time the result was failure, in most cases due to the senior marketing man's refusal to finalise the necessary agency agreement that I had arranged. On one occasion I had worked hard on the project and had been given to understand by an authoritative source on the Arabsat Board that if we could match the required specifications and put in a certain price in the region of $100 million then the contract would come to us, as it was considered that it was our turn to have it. I told the finance director about this and he did some sums and told me that he could meet the figure and would put the bid in accordingly, so I assumed we were home and dry this time. But when the time came to put in the bid to the Arabsat board who were due to meet in Amman, a senior director came out to Jordan bringing the bid with him and it turned out that the price quoted was about $5 million more than the agreed figure. In vain, I suggested that he should alter the figure in the offer and tried to convince him that the figure was a clerical error, but he would not do that. So the board met, decided to give the contract to our competitors and dispersed. I protested to the finance director, who said he was sorry and asked me to submit the bid again at the agreed price, but the decision had been taken and that was that. When I next met the man who had given me the winning price he said he was sorry but that we had 'kicked an own goal'! I found this most depressing and when it happened I went to bed determined to resign in the morning. However, I changed my mind over breakfast, thinking that it would be a stupid thing to do, and have never regretted it.

Another example of shortcomings in the overseas marketing of BAe products concerned Jordan and a new development of the Rapier low level anti-aircraft missile system which was Tracked Rapier, a version of the system mounted on a light tank chassis. The BAe people at Bristol had been working hard on this for some time and I talked about it in the Jordan Army HQ. The Army Commander, the Sharif Zaid bin Shaker, expressed interest and said he would like a demonstration in Jordan. I then went to the Ambassador to get his support for the project and he asked me if I could guarantee that such a demonstration would be a success. I felt a bit disloyal to the company but decided I had to say that I could not guarantee that there would be no hitches, but that if two equipments were brought out it should ensure success. I therefore suggested that he should use his influence to persuade people back home to do it that way. He agreed and arrangements went ahead on that basis.

I briefed the marketing director on all this and said that there was no rush and no deadline. The important thing was obviously to make sure that the equipments were in perfect working order. This was of the utmost importance because King Hussain would almost certainly attend and any failure or breakdown would become widely known and could destroy any hope of selling the equipment in the area for a long time. So arrangements went ahead and I had no reason to expect that anything would go wrong.

It was not until the equipments arrived in Jordan, one Tracked Rapier and one towed version as a back up, that I learned that the people at home in Bristol had been working day and night under great pressure to repair and overhaul the tracked equipment in time for its departure. I learned that there had been only one Tracked Rapier available for the occasion and that it had recently been used for rough ground tests of the engine, gear train and suspension, tests that had subjected the radar, computers and all the other electronics to a considerable beating. All those parts had therefore needed a thorough overhaul. Bristol had told the marketing director this and had pleaded for more time, only to be told that it was impossible to change the date and that they must do the best they could. In fact a postponement with reasonable notice would have been no problem in Jordan, but it was now too late for that and so the demonstration went ahead.

The local preparations were complete. A large marquee had been put up for the onlookers and the air force had been briefed to fly sorties so that the Rapier weapons could go through the motions of engaging them and demonstrating the mutual support which Rapier fire units were trained to give each other. King Hussain and a large number of staff and air defence officers were to attend.

The result was disaster. The towed equipment performed well but the Tracked Rapier vehicle broke down right in front of the stand and emitted a cloud of black smoke. The onlookers could see straight into the cab where an obviously panicking crew were vainly trying to get their equipment to perform as it should. They failed completely. The vehicle remained stationary and the missile launcher remained locked in its travelling position and refused to deploy itself for action. Our commentator, an instructor from the School of Anti-Aircraft Artillery, manfully endeavoured to divert the attention of the onlookers to what was happening as the other Rapier unit engaged the air force aircraft manoeuvring above them, but he could do little to retrieve the situation. With only one Rapier unit in action the concept of mutual support between fire units was completely lost and it was plain that the two aircraft attacking that unit had the best of the engagement. So the onlookers left, Zaid bin Shaker remarking politely that "Perhaps we will be able to see this equipment again when you have perfected it".

That particular affair was an instance of the very different approaches to marketing overseas as between Hawker Siddeley and the British Aircraft Corporation. Hawker Siddeley used to appoint permanent Regional Executives round the world each covering a number of countries and I was one of those. BAC's method was quite different. They used to send people abroad temporarily when opportunities seemed favourable and withdraw them if nothing was achieved. I was told that it was Sir Arnold Hall's policy in Hawker Siddeley to bolster the position and local reputation of the REs by ensuring that they were perceived locally as influential and highly trusted senior members of the company who were always present at important meetings in their area and at the corresponding social occasions. For instance he would say to the RE, "Look George. you must be with me when I go and see the Air Force Commander and you and I will be on Christian name terms. This will tend to strengthen your reputation with him for the future. But remember that this stops when we are out of the building and there are no local people present!"

On the formation of British Aerospace the whole of BAC but only half of Hawker Siddeley came together since the other half of Hawker Siddeley had nothing to do with aircraft or missile manufacture. The result was that the preponderance of the senior positions in BAe went to BAC people and this was certainly so in the case of marketing. The BAC attitude to

Regional Executives prevailed and this became plain to me during the demonstration in Jordan. The marketing director came out and made no effort to make sure that I was present at important meetings. Usually I managed to get in on such occasions but that was not always possible. Certainly I was left out when the senior Jordanians arrived for the demonstration. I was amused when it came to the social side of the visit. The marketing director said to me at the end of work on the first day when there was a high level Jordanian reception that evening, "All right Tony. See you tomorrow." So I said, "Oh. Aren't you going to the party tonight?" "Yes, of course I am." "Well I'll see you there then." "Have you been invited?" "Of course I have. See you there". Then the next night the Ambassador gave a dinner party for the occasion and an identical conversation occurred again!

An incident that pleased me very much at the time occurred when another change of marketing director took place at home. It was at a stage when the development of the structure of BAe had been reached where all the aircraft production elements of Hawker Siddeley and BAC had been amalgamated into the BAe Aircraft Group and all the other products had been put together in the Dynamics Group. I was still technically a member of Dynamics and was administered by them, but had been working for some time for the Aircraft Group as well. The new marketing director of Dynamics rang me up and said he wanted me to move back to the UK. He said he was sorry, and I would lose some of my privileges, such as first class travel, but that is what he had decided. I said I would think about what he had proposed.

I thought about the problem for an hour or so and decided that whatever happened I would not move. I very much enjoyed my job and considered that I was doing it well, but could not do it nearly as well from the UK. I would rather find another job based in the Middle East. So I rang up Colin Chandler who was a Hawker Siddeley man and managing director of the Aircraft Group. I told him what had occurred and he said, "That's a pity, but never mind. You stay where you are and go on doing what you have been doing for us in the Aircraft Group." So I said, "That's fine. I'll most willingly do that. Thank you." I then rang the Dynamics marketing director and said, "I've thought about your suggestion and I'm sorry but I've decided that I shall not come back home to Dynamics." He said, "But you must. I've decided that." "No, I'm staying here in Amman." "But what are you going to do?" "I'm going to remain here and be Regional Executive for the Aircraft Group as I have in fact been doing for some time now."

"How do you know that you can do that?" "Colin Chandler has just told me so." At that he rather abruptly rang off.

About an hour later he rang again and said that he had discussed the matter with Colin Chandler and that, in the circumstances, I had better stay where I was in Amman and continue to work for both Dynamics and for the Aircraft Group. So that was that and my life returned to normal after a nasty moment. Thanks to Colin Chandler I stayed in my job in Amman until I retired at the age of 65 in 1989. Colin went on to great things, being Head of Defence Sales in the MoD and then head of Vickers and being knighted. I owe him a lot.

Despite all these criticisms I remain a firm admirer of BAe. Its products are unsurpassed technically and I made many good friends in its widely varied departments. I enjoyed taking senior company people round the area, fixing appointments and going with them to see the senior potential buyers of whatever equipment they wanted to sell. Sometimes they were not very good at producing a 'sales pitch' and there were even occasions when I found myself having to do nearly all the talking to some army or air force commander. An important exception was Admiral Lygo, the veteran naval airman who retired as Chief of the Naval Staff and became the head of the Dynamics Group of BAe. He could talk in detail and very effectively on all the products of all the different parts of the company and that made going with him to meetings a pleasure.

My contacts with the Arab world continued for some time after I returned to the UK in 1989. I remained a consultant to the BAe Space Division for three years and toured the Middle East several times on behalf of various British companies before finally retiring after another ten years. I feel very fortunate in having been able to lead a most interesting life in a fascinating area where I have made many friends.

CHAPTER 9

Looking Back

W e both, Tony Cawston and Mike Curtis, consider ourselves very fortunate to have served in the Army when we did, at a time when there were still different and stimulating extra-regimental military jobs available overseas, as opposed to the boring repetition of peacetime soldiering at home or in Germany. We have, of course, done our share of that as well, but our service in the Scouts was very different. There was the sense that we were doing something genuinely important and useful that could not be done sensibly in any other way. Britain had been in control of the Gulf for many years and many of the Gulf states had welcomed us in the area and had relied on us for their defence and for their foreign relations. But it was becoming clear that such a situation was going to have to come to an end and that we, the British, were therefore responsible for ensuring that the process of preparing the Gulf states for independence was properly carried out and put on to a firm and lasting basis. It was also, of course, very much in Britain's interest to ensure the continued stability of the Gulf as a major source of the supply of oil after the withdrawal of military forces.

It was plain that the individual Trucial States were too small, politically and economically, to survive as separate independent entities and so it became sensible to plan for a federation of the various sheikhdoms to ensure their future collective independence. At first a federation was envisaged of all the Gulf states for which Britain was responsible, to include Bahrain and Qatar as well as the seven Trucial States, but for various reasons the first two withdrew from the idea. In fact even amongst the remaining seven there was a reluctance to accept the idea of sacrificing sheikhly independence to the extent required for the formation of a federation and it was very largely due to the tireless efforts of the Political Agent in Dubai in the very early 1960s, Donald Hawley, with the support of the Political Resident in Bahrain, that this resistance was gradually overcome so that the federation of the United Arab Emirates was finally formed in December 1971. Latterly, Sir Geoffrey Arthur, who had been ambassador in Kuwait, became the PR in Bahrain and it was then largely due to his diplomatic skills that the Rulers were finally persuaded to sign the union agreement. At the same time the Trucial Oman Scouts became the Union Defence Force, eventually merging with the more recently formed Abu Dhabi Defence Force a few years later to form the bulk of the UAE Armed Forces.

The Trucial Oman Scouts, however, had played a very significant part in this achievement at a lower level. The very fact that, at grass root level, it was the Scouts who built up the peaceable relationship between the sheikhdoms contributed to the eventual general acceptance of the idea that some sort of federation with the Scouts as the foundation of a federal army was the way forward. Two other factors were very significant in the progress towards federation. The first was the confirmation that great reserves of oil existed in the area and the consequent first payments by the oil companies for their concessions. The second was the character and drive of Sheikh Zayed of Abu Dhabi. Zayed as the younger brother of Sheikh Shakhbut, the Ruler of Abu Dhabi, was the governor of the Abu Dhabi part of the Buraimi oases and was also, in tribal terms, the most important sheikh of the area including tribes in the nearby parts of Omani territory. He was widely revered, not least by the officers of the TOS, as a man with the leadership qualities which were likely to be needed in the future. It became obvious that Sheikh Shakhbut was not the man to oversee the development of his sheikhdom which was now possible and desirable due to the increasing oil revenues. So it was decided that his brother Zayed should replace him, but that bloodshed must be avoided. A coup was carefully planned with Zayed's agreement and was put into effect in 1966 with a Scouts operation in which Mike Curtis' 'A' Squadron played a major part. The change of Ruler was immediately accepted by all concerned, including not much later, by Shakhbut himself.

So their period in the Scouts was a rewarding experience for the British who served there and they all felt that they were achieving something of value to their own country and to the local people of the area. The same applied to the officers who served in the Sultan's Armed Forces, as Tony Cawston was fortunate enough for a short time to do. So, we, these two Scouts, consider that we were very lucky in our periods of service to have had the opportunity to serve in the TOS and take part in the development of an area and society based on an ancient civilisation where we made many friends.

Part Two

THE LIFE
AND TIMES
OF A
SCOUTS OFFICER
1966–1968

CHAPTER 1

How it all begun

I had left school in 1957 and had been fortunate enough to get a sort of apprenticeship with EMI Records (HMV, Columbia, Parlophone), which meant living in digs in Hayes, Middlesex and learning absolutely everything about the gramophone record industry. It included visits to Abbey Road studios where I met most of the recording stars of the time. I knew I would have to do National Service at some time, and it came as no surprise to me to get a summons from the Company Personnel Department who told me that I should have registered. There then followed the business of interviews and medicals and in early 1959 I caught a train from Salisbury to take me to Exeter.

I thoroughly enjoyed joining the Army and being subjected to basic training at Wessex Brigade as most of the staff were from Devon and Dorset – genuine country lad types. Having been shunted around from Exeter to the War Office Selection board and eventually to Mons Officer Cadet School at Aldershot, I was commissioned into the regiment of my choice, The Royal Hampshire Regiment, in December 1959. I was very lucky and was posted to the rifle company being sent to Nassau in the Bahamas.

We sailed from Southampton in the troopship Dunera which took the best part of a month to get into the West Indies. This included a day at Las Palmas in the Canaries to take on more water! There followed the long haul across the Atlantic to Port of Spain in Trinidad where our 'A' Company was flown to Georgetown, British Guyana and a Worcesters' company was taken on board. While this was going on the rest of us spent two days surfing at Maracas Beach and enjoying our first visit to the West Indian culture. After three or four days we arrived at Kingston, Jamaica, a very busy port, where our HQ Company plus Battalion Headquarters and Support Company disembarked. Similar Worcester companies were taken on board.

A quick trip across to a point about 5 miles off Belize (because of the coral reefs) was made to swap over rifle companies. A return to Kingston changed over the resident rifle companies and a glorious cruise to Nassau followed. During most of this period we had to stay on board Dunera and we were relieved to see the City of Nassau one morning through our portholes. Our 'Y' Company took over Oakesfield camp from the Worcesters and we started at last to settle down.

My job in 'Y' Company was Reserve Platoon Commander and presented no real hardships, it was just very boring as I was also an administrative assistant to the Second in Command. All was peace and quiet for the first 3–4 months until an internal uprising in Jamaica indicated that we had a job to do in bringing peace to that island. The revolutionaries were part of the Return to Africa movement who had been promised the return to their homeland if they voted in a certain Prime Minister. History has it that the gentleman had been elected but there was no boat provided for them to go home in – hence the uprising. After about one month when two of our chaps were killed in action, things quietened down. My two years National Service came to an end in January 1961. I returned to 'Civvy Street'.

Working back at Hayes with EMI was very dull in comparison to the previous two years but I struggled on for four months. I finally realised that I would like to return to the Army (much against my father's will) and rejoin my regiment. As no further reinforcements were being sent to the West Indies I was posted to Salisbury Plain as Continuation Training Officer with the Duke of Edinburgh's Royal Regiment. I spent the best part of a year and a half carrying out training with new drafts from the Depot. This was enormously satisfying, especially when a team of 12 Fijians turned up, some of the first to join the British Army. Not only were they very keen and fit soldiers but they were also excellent rugger players, helping the battalion win the area cup.

The Duke of Edinburgh's were off to Malta in late 1962 and I was posted to Wessex Brigade Depot at Honiton, Devon. This was the raw edge of training soldiers, very interesting and sometimes rewarding, but not helped by senior officers who suffered from small doses of humanity. Whilst I was there we endured the worst winter for many years, almost snowbound most of the time. Emergency deliveries of hay to stranded cattle were our main task, giving recruits exciting work in helicopters. After a short stay I was posted to my regiment in Munster, Germany. The atmosphere was totally different, with much emphasis being spent on what to do if the Russians crossed the River Weser. Exercise after exercise, lasting in some cases up to a month, in a really useless vehicle called the Humber one ton armoured (Pig), which on its own would have given the Russians a clear run to Ostend.

In the autumn exercise of 1964, a young university entry officer was accidentally killed when one of these infamous Pigs rolled on him and killed him. As he was newly married and due to take up the gentle posting of recruiting officer in Winchester, the line of least resistance swung my way as I lived nearby. I agreed to do the job providing it was for six months only, which would give me time to attend pre-course training for the Support Platoon Commander's course. This was agreed and noted in my Personal File.

During 1965 in Winchester I awaited the call to do this course, but I received not one word from the Commanding Officer in Munster, in spite of his agreement earlier. In the end I did over a year in the job and did not get my Support Platoon Commander's posting. The Battalion went off to the Indonesian Confrontation emergency, leaving me on gardening leave. I was beginning to think perhaps I had made the wrong decision in rejoining the Army. As one got older there seemed to be more really inept commanders at all levels knocking about.

After an attempt to get me to go to Zambia (which I refused) I was posted to Aden to learn Arabic prior to being posted to the Trucial Oman Scouts. It is well known that this language is one of the hardest known to man and I certainly had not volunteered for such a posting.

CHAPTER 2

Arrival at Aden, Arabic language school

I had left the peace and tranquillity of my family home in Hampshire on a rather wet and cold day in January 1966 to go to Gatwick on my way to Aden. I had been sent a ticket and instructions for me to report to the Gatwick Air Trooping Centre where I was to catch a British United Airways VC10 to Aden. This was one of the Army trooping contracts that existed at the time and British United had the lion's share of the contract.

When I got to Gatwick, I didn't actually know anybody at all from my own regiment or from my own part of the country except possibly one and that was Graham Tullet who was a Worcester but lived in Chichester. We all climbed on board this VC10 and started talking amongst ourselves and discussing where our various battalions had been and what we had done in our military careers. At the time I was 25. The journey soon went by; it was non-stop across Europe down the coast of Italy, over Egypt and down the Red Sea into Aden. We arrived round about midnight and it seemed steaming hot and very humid to us chaps from England. We were met at the foot of the steps of the aircraft by an extraordinary fellow, Major Dick Cross Kelly, from the Royal Ulster Rifles, who was the Admin Officer of the Arabic School.

I think I should make it quite clear at this stage that I had no wish, desire or inclination to serve with foreign troops. Anyone who serves with foreign troops has to be interviewed by an officer not below the rank of Major General to confirm that he is suitable for service with foreign troops. I had not been interviewed by anybody and had to assume that there had been a mistake made at Exeter where they had tried to shove me off just anywhere after the Zambia question. I had no previous entries on my confidential report that suggested that I had requested service with foreign troops, let alone learn Arabic. This all probably cost the Ministry of Defence a considerable sum of money. If anybody had taken the trouble to look at my scholastic record, which was available to them, they would have found that I got 8% 'O' level oral French and about 25% in the written exam, making it quite clear to all and sundry that I was really not a linguist. I was simply an infantry officer who had done his National Service with his county regiment and decided to sign on. I had been cooperative and accommodating and agreed to do the recruiting job after a brother officer had been killed, after which all assurances for my future career were ignored.

So, sending me to Aden to learn a language which was totally different to English and French and expect me to show an inclination to passing exams in it was not a very wise decision on the part of senior officers. I was completely dumbfounded by all this, I had no interest in it and I had really no desire to go. The situation in Aden at the time was one of riots, shooting, bombs and internal security problems. This was the sort of thing I was really trained to deal with but, instead of being given a rifle, I was given a pen and I was shoved in the annex of the Crescent Hotel at Steamer Point, sharing a room with another officer, where we both had to struggle to learn Arabic for three months.

Our day was a simple affair; we woke at 5.30am or thereabouts; we had breakfast in the main part of the hotel and a series of Land Rovers (without armed guards and driven, would you believe it, by Adeni locals) came and took us from Steamer Point to Waterloo Lines where the school was located. I can remember two of the teachers there; one was Owen Taylor who was really a most sympathetic career officer who had in fact been with the Trucial Oman Scouts at some stage and I rather wished I had had him as my tutor. My actual tutor was a little chap called Bernard Smith, who tried very hard, but I don't think he had come across reluctant heavy infantry officers before. Around about lunchtime we were sent back to the hotel, where we had lunch and had the afternoon and evening to ourselves. This normally meant that we went down to Tarshine Beach which was the Officers Club, where we had a swim and a cup of tea each day and sat down to learn twenty-five words in Arabic. We were given cards the size of visiting cards, on one side we wrote the English and on the other side we wrote the transliterated Arabic. If we were lucky in the evening we managed to get dinner in the hotel and if we were unlucky we were clobbered to work a radio in the Joint Security Centre which was right behind the Hotel.

I don't really remember too many interesting incidents from this time except that some nights we went across to Flints Island in the harbour at Aden which was inhabited by some Australian architects. Here we had a few beers and a laugh or two and we came back at about 10 p.m. One evening as we climbed the steps from the boat, we found that Steamer Point was in the grip of a massive cordon and search operation and we nearly got arrested for being out during curfew. On another occasion, I

Tarshine Beach, Aden

remember going to have a curry supper with Bernard Smith, my tutor, where there were three or four of us in his flat in Murder Mile in Maalla. A blindicide (rocket) went off from Jebel Shamsan at the back and went straight through a house not far from us and exploded in the harbour.

The Ministry of Defence, or Middle East Command at the time I suppose, realised that there was an awful lot of money being spent on twenty or so officers in the hotel and when there was room we got moved into the Officers Mess in Singapore Lines, which was in effect the Aden Brigade Officers Mess. This was a great big open rambling colonial type building, some parts of which were air conditioned, most weren't, where we were given a room in a small annex.

It made life a lot harder for us after this move because when we wanted to go to Tarshine we had to take a taxi, which again was a considerable risk and which was expensive to go all the way down to Steamer Point and back again. I can remember being fed up by all this and getting nowhere with the Arabic and I did a considerable amount of damage riding around the Officers Mess ante-room on a scooter. I then leant out of an upstairs window one night and purely by accident knocked a window air conditioner off the wall. It fell to the ground outside and narrowly missed the Force dentist, who accused me of trying to murder him. Finally

102

Colonel Freddie de Butts

towards the end of all this nonsense, Tom Gibson, Brigade Major of Aden Brigade (who was from the Duke of Edinburgh's Royal Regiment) called me in and said that I was really particularly evil and that I had better start knuckling under. I told him the full story of how I had ended up in Aden and he said "You have been very badly handled; I think we had better go to the General".

103

The next thing I knew I was being interviewed by Lieutenant General Sir John Willoughby, one of the nicest officers I think I have ever met, who had a Lt. Colonel with him who, again, was remarkably sympathetic. The whole of my story went out to him and he said "there is not an awful lot I can do, you either stick it and go to the Scouts, or, if not, you have to go back to England and you may end up almost anywhere. You certainly could not go on to Singapore to meet up with your Battalion, even though there is a VC10 going through Aden each week to Gan and Singapore". Anyway, he said that he understood that they were now up to full strength. So, as the 3 months had almost come to the end, I thought I might as well have a look at the Scouts. I was still fed up, uninterested, itching to have a go in an Aden-type situation, but I had to accept the facts.

The course came to an end and suddenly word was about that the Commander of the Scouts was in Aden; his name was Colonel Freddie De Butts, and he was from the Light Infantry. So having said to the General that I would go to the Scouts, I remembered one small piece of help he gave me. He said: "If you find it totally impossible up there and alien to anything that you wish to do, you can send me a cable". Quite clearly Freddie de Butts had come down to Aden to see if I was worthy of even being put on an Argosy to go to Sharjah. However, in the end I packed my gear and got on the plane, which was on the milk run from Aden to Bahrain. Freddie De Butts was one of the few allowed a seat at the back; the rest of us had to sit in parachute string seats for most of the day. We flew from Aden to Salalah, where we had a cup of coffee while they refuelled the aircraft. Then we flew on to Sharjah, and arrived late one afternoon in early April 1966. Throughout the whole trip Freddie De Butts had not said a word to me, except in the Officers Mess at Salalah where he said: "Ah, you're Curtis are you?" and I said "Yes sir," and he replied "I will see you in Sharjah tomorrow," and that is all that was said.

CHAPTER 3

Joining the Trucial Oman Scouts

When I arrived at Sharjah one person was there to meet me whom I had met before, a rather large Scottish officer who was soon to become known as the Laird, one John Whitelaw. He took me and my kit up to the Officers Mess and introduced me to the Scouts officers. They seemed an exciting lot; some were hiding from messy divorces, some were long term bachelors and some were pushing up the shares of the various beer and whisky brands. There were one or two career officers there who were coming in to do staff jobs, do them well and then move on. And there were one or two, who, like me, had just been snowballed into it or who had actually volunteered for it.

I had about four days in Sharjah and was told very quickly that I was to be Second in Command of 'A' Squadron, under a Royal Highland Fusilier called Dennis Halstead. The Squadron was then based in the wilderness, at a place called Mirfa, which was miles to the west – halfway to the Qatar/Trucial States border – and east of Jebel Dhanna. During these four days I had to get myself kitted out with the local uniform, I had been promoted from Lieutenant to Captain and had to get myself an orderly. The Mess Staff Sergeant was a man called Mohammed Iqbal, a Baluchi from

Ruler's Palace, Sharjah

Sharjah and he had lined up against the wall a dozen or so cronies from the Sharjah Souk from whom I could choose an orderly. I asked if any of them had had any previous military experience, and a man called Said Alam Khan Afridi from North West Pakistan produced his end of service book, which was similar to the old British book. He had been in the South Waziristan Scouts at some stage, so seeing that his character had been attested as being exemplary, I took him on. He was very thin and emaciated and about six feet tall. Off he went to the Doctor to be checked out and declared free from infection and I went to see the force tailor to get some of the so-called grey musry shirts that one wore outside the trousers with a red stable belt and the traditional red shamagh with black headrope (agal). I was also kitted out with a really rather nice white mess kit and all the other bits and pieces which included a Camp Kit; Officers for the use of, which had everything in it from a bath to blankets and camp beds. These were to be part of my life for the next two years.

Having kitted myself out, I was then ready to go, but before I went I was summoned to be interviewed officially by the Commander. I entered, halted and saluted; I was not asked to stand at ease but was given a fairly strong broadside from the Colonel (i.e. the Commander, Freddie de Butts) and was not even allowed to speak. At the end I said, "Well Sir, I am not a volunteer, I have come here under duress, and if I don't fit I think I have the right to go home." And with that he said "You had better go and see what you are going to do with yourself." So I went out and the first person I bumped into after that was a very nice jovial chap, who was to become a great friend: Lt Col Bob Feltham of the Devon and Dorsets, whom I had first met when he was Second in Command of the Cheshires in Munster in the early sixties. His wife Liz was absolutely charming and they lived in one of the houses on Flagstaff Hill.

It was now time to get my first taste of Arabia and I left Sharjah, which in those days was the centre of most commercial and social activities; it had a creek and the first RAF airfield in the Gulf. Dubai in those days was just beginning to develop towards what it is today, the centre of that end of the Gulf. The reason why Sharjah became less favoured was because its creek silted up and most of the dhows chose to go into Dubai.

There was a system operating in this area and it probably still works, which says that when you left any location you put the number of your vehicle down, who was in it and what route you were taking, to be transmitted to the next location. The principle was that when you got to the other end, you checked your presence into the radio office and the two messages (one outgoing from Sharjah and the other incoming from Mirfa, or wherever), were pinned together and the Duty Officer then knew that there was nobody lost – a very good idea and used extensively. The reason for this was that there were no roads; we drove over sand or gravel tracks; the maps were rudimentary; there was little other traffic and, with the intense summer heat, there was the danger of suffering from heat stroke if the vehicle had broken down. Another interesting point here is that the radios we used did not have the range for voice except under exceptional conditions, so Morse code was used. The Morse code operators were in the main teenage Arab boys of about the age of 16 when they were recruited, trained in the boys' school and then sent to the various parts of the force. They knew no English, but were trained to listen to the Morse message and write an English capital letter for each Morse letter. These operators were very proficient at sending Morse messages from the back of Land Rovers, even when bouncing across the desert during exercises.

So we set off in two Dodge Power Wagons. This is a rather large 4×4 open wagon, two seats in the front, cargo carrying space in the back with a powerful winch on the front, which could also be used through the chassis to the back and it had huge balloon tyres. These two trucks were filled with rice, dates, flour and whatever else was needed in Mirfa and my

Mirfa Camp

suitcases and bedding roll were unceremoniously tossed into the back. We set off from Sharjah across the sabhka, the salt marsh that exists all along that end of the Gulf Coast, which is where the salt water comes up under the sand and makes it very boggy and very smelly. The Scouts had a system whereby each Squadron rotated around the locations every six months and this was called 'roundabout'. Like a bunch of gypsies, you loaded everything into the Bedfords and moved on to the next place.

We set off pretty early and went around the back of Dubai and down the Jumeira Beach road, where it ended not far from where the Jumeira Beach Hotel is now, and then across the Jebel Ali bombing range, which is now a huge man-made harbour. After a long flog we ended up at the Abu Dhabi coffee shop which is where the road from Abu Dhabi to Al Ain and Buraimi crosses the road from Dubai to Mirfa. We stopped there for the soldiers to pray and have a bit of lunch, which I seem to remember was a rather tired sandwich and a cup of cold sweet tea, after which we set off for Tarif. After another two to three hours we came down a track to Tarif, the centre of the oil drilling area of the Abu Dhabi Petroleum Company, which was the main reason why we had a squadron down there, and at about tea time we arrived at Mirfa. After crossing a large dusty plain we came over a Jebel (Arabic for mountain/hill) and there below me was a tented camp, almost like Lawrence of Arabia's, on the edge of the sea. I was hot, pretty frustrated, fed up, tired and the thought of the humid and hot existence that awaited me here filled me with complete horror. However, here was Dennis, a sunburnt, cheerful Scotsman and the first thing he offered me was a cool drink so I thought, "Well, this man knows the form," and I had a rather late lunch in the mess tent.

The mess tent consisted of a bar at one end, a small dining room and some rather rotten old armchairs. The sleeping accommodation was in three small ex-oil company cabins which had window-banger air conditioners. These only worked when the generator worked, which was part of the desalination plant. This operated from 8–10 p.m., so we went to bed early and started the night cool. The lavatorial arrangements were somewhat primitive in that about 50 yards from the mess tent there was a desert rose and on the edge of the sea was a barasti hut with a flagpole. You waded through the deep puffy sand to the water's edge every morning, but you made sure that you put the flag up when you were in there, because nobody was going to walk all that way and stand in the sun waiting for you.

We had, I think, about a month or two in Mirfa, during which time I had

Dennis Halstead and Scouts

to learn the patrolling routes, the various oil fields, the rigs, the pipelines, the tracks that were leading towards the Liwa (an area of deep sand dunes, between the oil fields and the Saudi border) and the oil port at Jebel Dhanna. It was a place to go and have an air conditioned curry and on occasions Dennis and I used to drive to Tarif where we had a friend called Bob Foster who worked for Santa Fe Drilling. He would give us a very good meal and we would end up by going back to his cabin for a coffee and a movie. Tarif was a camp surrounded by oil drums. When we left at night, whoever was sober, had to count the 24th oil drum from the right and go between that and the 25th. You then held the steering wheel absolutely rock steady for twenty-eight minutes and if you were lucky you came over the edge of the scarp into Mirfa. We did this a number of times.

During this time at Mirfa I remember that my attitude towards the Scouts started to change and it was mostly down to understanding Dennis. I was beginning, I think, to address myself to the business of soldiering, even though my Arabic was still appalling. I had failed the exam in Aden without much difficulty and they then said I would have to take it again in Sharjah in six months' time, in order that I might get my £100 for my linguist Grade 4. Anyway a sergeant was put to teach me the various local words in Arabic and to learn some conversational pieces. His name was Sgt Abdullah Gadaya, the light troop sergeant, who over the years was to become a close friend of mine. He finished his military career as a Defence Attache for the Emirates in Khartoum, Sudan.

So there we were, down in the far west, miles away from anywhere, going through Bu Hasa and Habshan (two operating bases for the oil fields) every second week or so, patrolling to make sure that all was well. It is interesting to note that when our desalination plant broke down, our Bedford 4 ton bowser had to drive fifty miles to Bu Hasa to get water and fifty miles back. After two months of this, we were at 'roundabout' and we set off to move the whole squadron to become resident squadron in Sharjah, nearer the hub of things and where there was more officialdom. I was told that there would be a good bit of public duties for the squadron when we were there. I was sent ahead with the advance party and the thought of having an air conditioned kip, let alone the use of air conditioned lavatory arrangements, was exciting and foremost in my mind.

Two characters in 'A' Squadron were very kind, very cooperative and generally extremely friendly. The senior Arab officer, a man called Hassan Said who commanded the Light Troop, was very helpful in teaching me Arabic as we went along. The other two Troops were commanded by Sergeants, as there were no other officers around at the time. The Squadron Sergeant-Major was Atiq bin Murad, who strangely enough I see a good

Atiq bin Murad

deal of, even today. He retired eventually from the Abu Dhabi Navy in the rank of Lieutenant-Colonel or equivalent and is now a well settled property owner in Al Ain. The rest of the Squadron were a mixture from the various tribes, the Beni Kaab, the Kitbis, the Dhofaris, the Balouch and some Indians in administrative positions. The Dhofaris were a very war-like and proficient race and excellent soldiers. They came from the country around Salalah, the capital of Dhofar, which is the south-western part of the Sultanate of Oman. We recruited them every year on the principle that they signed on for a three year contract and, after two years nine months, they were allowed to go on leave and, if they didn't come back, we reckoned that we had had our money's worth and nothing was lost. They all signed on for Her Majesty the Queen. It is interesting to note that when we had Squadron Orders and blokes were fined for misbehaviour, it was a question of a 10 rupee fine and 10 rupees for Her Majesty. Everything was divided into two. They all took it extremely well, all realising that they were working for the British Government.

It is worthy of note that, at this stage, the Trucial Oman Scouts were officered by the British Army, with British NCOs in various senior ranks at HQ. It was a Foreign Office force under the direction of the Political Resident in Bahrain who, when I got there, was Sir William Luce. The funds for it came entirely from the Foreign Office and it was a force that was put together to patrol and police the Trucial States. It was originally called the Trucial Oman Levies and, as it got bigger, it became the Trucial Oman Scouts.

CHAPTER 4

Roundabout back to Sharjah

Ispent my first real night under the stars with my advance party some four miles south of Jumeirah towards Jebel Ali, where we waited to enter Sharjah the next morning to take over from the Resident Squadron in the camp complex. This we duly did and I moved up to the Resident Squadron's Second-in-Command's bedroom where everything was prepared for me; a decent bed, air conditioning, showers and baths and lavatories with lavatory paper – all terribly nice. We got the advance party settled in and two days later the main party drove in. We then spent the best part of a week or so getting the squadron in, the weapons checked, the vehicles checked and everything cleaned up, so that we could change our role from being Scouts or border patrollers to becoming almost a squadron for ceremonial duties.

It is interesting here when I mention the word 'Scouting' to tell the story of a chap I met way down below the old French road, on the edge of the Liwa, that leads to the oilfields. He was a chap called Martin Buckmaster who worked for the Political Agent in Dubai who, in those days, was a charming Welsh man called David Roberts. Martin's job was to map out the various areas, taking into account tribal affinity and allegiances. He had a very simple system. Every time he came to a change in direction he put a bit of steel scaffolding with a very large cement weight into the ground, another one ten yards back in the direction of the previous marker and another one ten yards forward in the direction of travel so, lining up two of these steel poles indicated the direction of either the last or the next boundary change. In the end all the tribes recognised and accepted Martin's border rules and a really significant development it was to bringing stability to the area. Some years later, having left the Scouts and entered civilian employment with Boots the Chemist in Beirut, I next saw Martin, when my wife and I were pushing a pram along a rocky footpath near Pigeon Rock. He suddenly appeared and remembered me, so much so that he asked us for Christmas dinner in his lovely house in Patriarcat. He retired and inherited his father's title of Viscount, having done some time in the British Embassy in Yemen.

The arrival into Sharjah meant that I came into contact with the force

HQ, which had a motley array of staff officers. As I explained, Freddie de Butts was the Commander, Bob Feltham was the Deputy Commander and the G2 (Grade 2 Staff Officer) was Ray Shotter from the Royal Engineers. His G3 (Grade 3 Staff Officer) was John Whitelaw whose main job, seemed to be tasking helicopters, aircraft and allotting ranges. He was working for his staff college exam at the time. The Force Intelligence Officer was a little gunner major called Tim (Meredith) Budd who had his ear to the ground (if he could get it there!) it is claimed. He was well known for the noise he made whilst eating, especially soup.

The DQ (Deputy Assistant Adjutant Quartermaster General – responsible for manning and supplies) was a most amusing major from the Royal Tank Regiment called David Glazebrook, with whom I was later to have dinner in the early 1970s, when he was Defence Attaché in Khartoum for the British Government. His Staff Captain was a most amazing chap called John Pitt who was a paratrooper from the Royal Corps of Transport and who was to become a very close friend in the years to come. (He retired with the rank of Brigadier some years ago and later became the Director of Sports Amenities for Wandsworth, where he said he was earning more than he did as a brigadier! We had lunch with Desmond Cosgrove, a very competent Arabist who had held many important positions in the Gulf some years ago and we could have gone on talking for 3 days.)

That was force HQ, such as it was. The Prison Officer (we had the only

Sharjah Creek, 1966

prison on the coast in those days) was Jack Briggs who eventually ended up establishing and building the Dubai Police Force for Sheikh Rashid bin Said al Makhtoum, the ruler of Dubai. Jack retired more than once and did noble work in Dubai. The force doctor was Peter Swinhoe, a career doctor, who joined the Scouts after a long period as a GP. He ended up as a brigadier and I think was one of the doctors to her Majesty the Queen at some stage. George Cornish ran the REME workshops, with Cliff Squires as his number two, whilst Richard Wallace ran the Supply and Transport Squadron, with Simon Swindells from the Royal Corps of Transport as his number two. David Morris ran the Signals, with Ian Crouch as his second in command and Tim Ash as warrant officer. Ian Crouch was later to become a Lt Colonel. That was basically the staff in Sharjah. On one side of the square was the force HQ, on another the Force Mosque and on the southside were situated HQ Squadron and the Resident Squadron. Between us and the airfield there was a NAAFI shop and, having wended your way through our logistics lines, you arrived at RAF station Sharjah which was a staging post, where visiting squadrons of Hunters and Canberras came for practical training.

We were now in an area of responsibility that stretched from the Abu Dhabi coffee shop right up the coast to Ras Al Khaimah and inland to the Hajar mountains. Part of the responsibilities of the Resident Squadron was that the Squadron Commander became the President of the Mess Committee of the Officers Mess and the Second in Command became the

Dennis Halstead at the Scouts' stables

Parade taken by Political Agent, David Roberts

food member, which I suppose was a bit of a swindle in many ways, because there were enough staff officers around who could have done the job just as well and provided better continuity. But it was interesting that I should take on this job, as I used to go down to the shop in Sharjah called Spinneys, where I met a young Lebanese manager called David Eid. At that time, ie 1966, he was a very young manager. He was later the General Manager of the Spinneys company in Doha, Qatar, when I was General Manager of the Spinneys company in Muscat and we used to sit for long hours at conferences talking about the old days of Sharjah.

The Mess was really one central building where there was the bar, the dining room, the ante rooms and the kitchens. Off one side there was the junior officers' annex and at the other side there was the senior officers' annex, which consisted of a bedroom and a sitting room each. One of the characters of the mess was the Paymaster, Major Don Tibby, an officer who was known as 'Father', who in the bar had his own seat with a brass plaque behind it. He had been the Paymaster for many many years, could drink almost anybody under the table and even had a fridge in his bedroom, where he used to keep the odd crate to revitalise his soul. 'Father' left the Scouts, handed over to a chap called Bob Bedford and went to the Pay Office at Wrexham which he didn't like at all. He got the chance to go back to Sharjah as the Paymaster for British Troops, at the time that they took over the Mess from the Scouts. I am told he sat in his old chair again and it is with much sadness that we learnt that he had died some 15 or so years ago of a stroke. He was buried in the small Christian Churchyard in Sharjah behind the Resident Squadron lines. Many years later when I went back to Sharjah, as number two in Spinneys, I went up one afternoon to have a look around and I found his grave, the discovery of which is related later.

We did quite a lot of patrolling out of Sharjah, most of which was down Jebel Ali way. There was a water pipeline that ran up from inland Sharjah, which we had to check every now and then, and of course there were certain elements of recreation that one didn't have in other outstations. For example there was a sailing club and we had a superb mounted Squadron of the most wonderful Arab stallions, under the command of the Force dentist, who was Captain Andrew Young of the Royal Army Dental Corps. We were able to use these horses in the evenings to go up the coast. Andrew used to appear on serious parades with the horses beautifully turned out, with the Scouts guidon, which had a bright green background with golden embroidered crossed khunjas and cannon barrels, like the cap badge, in the middle of it. Andrew was a good dentist and I can report that he was an expert on bicycling the drill to get the appropriate revs up to do a bit of teeth drilling when around the outstations.

The mounted Squadron was managed by Sergeant Wilson from the Life Guards, who kept the place absolutely spotless. I had a horse allocated to me called Commando and for the first and last time in my life I took up riding. They tried to teach me tent pegging and polo, but I was best at just riding up the beach towards Ajman, just before the sun went down. These trips were great fun as I used to be accompanied by Dennis Halstead and

'A' Squadron practices air portability

John Whitelaw. I remember on one occasion, John's stirrup leather broke and he went hurtling past me horizontally and was very badly grazed. We used to come back and hose the horses off (rather like hosing off a Land Rover) and the syces used to cool them and dry them down. We then repaired to the bar which was known as the 'Jolly Bedu' where we could have a pint or two before dinner. It was outside this that I again bumped into Liz Feltham who was a most wonderful person and had a very lively sense of humour.

Rugby football was introduced here at this time and I was chosen to play in one of the few games in the Trucial States, when we took on Dubai. We had a pitch that was raked sabkha, just down from the RAF camp, and the team that we played was known as the Dubai Rugby Football Club, now known as the Dubai Exiles, and John Pitt and others, myself included, bandaged ourselves from head to foot, like Michelin men, to play Rugby on this very rough sandpaper-like surface. I cannot remember who won, but I am pretty sure there was a lot of beer consumed afterwards.

It was at this stage that we managed to get another officer, a chap called Salim bin Mussalim al Said, who was a Dhofari and had been a Qaid's commissioned officer (locally commissioned). He had proved his worth and had gone to Mons Officer Cadet School and arrived back and been given the Queen's Commission and became Troop Leader of number two Troop. He was a very good keen young officer from Salalah, not a member of the Omani Royal Family even though his name was similar. Later when I got command of the squadron, I watched him very carefully and I recommended that he should go on one more step and do the mortar course. In due course he passed this course and after I had left the Scouts, he returned to Sharjah and joined Support Squadron. Support Squadron was based at Manama and in my day was commanded by a chap called David Neild, who was originally from RCT, but had transferred to the Kings Regiment. He was a great friend of Desmond Cosgrove's, who had been in the Scouts before I got there, and he had an infamous old orderly called Gus who was quite the most frightening creature known to man, a bit like Quasimodo! He always had a pistol in his belt and one wondered what was going to happen next; he could not cook, but he kept David in good order.

There were two bits of excitement when we were in Sharjah. The first was the currency change and the second was the removal of Sheikh Shakhbut from power in Abu Dhabi. At that time, there were two basic currencies in use; one was the Reserve Bank of India rupee and the second was the Bahraini dinar in use in Abu Dhabi. There were also a lot of Qatar

Dubai clock tower

rials about and it was a complete mess. It was decided that we should go
through a system, whereby we would have to start with a Qatar/Dubai rial,
on the way to having some form of standard currency. Unfortunately, this
resulted in riots in Sharjah souk and I had to take half a Squadron down
to make sure that when people went to change their money it was done
without too much shouting. This was a nasty incident, which I took care
of, and it took some considerably time to quieten the crowds down. In the
end, peace and stability came to Sharjah. One of my soldiers asked for
special leave to get his money from his village. The notes had been buried
in an earthenware pot under his burasti. In his absence his wife had moved
the burasti and the money was never found – a sad, amusing incident.

At one end of the souk there was a small silversmith called Adam
Sheikh Na'im, an Iraqi who had an amusing nick-name. He used to make
the most superb silver ashtrays to take home as presents for the girlfriends
and he also made some very good gold and silver khunja brooches.

On the lighter side of life we put together something called the Raises'
(Captains') Union, which was a collection of the junior officers, who every

118

Deira side of Dubai creek

now and then had a party on a beach some way away and invited all the old and bold along to a BBQ put up by the Mess Sergeant and his team. Life flashed by rather quickly towards August 1966 and I had been out on patrol for a week or two, had come in, had a good shower, a kip and a decent meal and I was playing Mickey Mouse darts in the Jolly Bedu, and was told that the operation to remove Sheikh Shakhbut was being planned. This is explained in greater detail in the next chapter.

I ought to explain that Dubai was a good way across the salt plains from Sharjah and was the only place we could go for any form of extra activity, or to see anything approaching civilisation. We used to go therefore, only about once a week, to the Old Bustan Hotel and the Riviera Hotel on the Creek. I remember one such occasion when the local branch of the Buffalos were having an evening session on the balcony of the Bustan Hotel. I believe the Chairman was our RSM (Nicholas from the Coldstream Guards) and they were having a raffle for a motor car. So we all ended up there hoping to be able to purchase a raffle ticket or two, but unsurprisingly we did not win. As we left the Bustan it was possible in those days to cross straight across the runway and through some small sand dunes before meeting the main track. It just happened to be the one day in the week when the VC10 was coming in from London and it had to abort its landing, as 6 Land Rovers hurtled across the runaway on their way back to Sharjah. Next morning we were hauled up in front of the Political Agent and the Commander and given one hell of a dressing down. It was on August 6th whilst having another go at Mickey Mouse (a type of darts game) and winning, that I was called to an Orders Group at 0100hrs in the morning for details of one of the most momentous tasks in the history of the Scouts.

CHAPTER 5

The Day that reshaped the Gulf

Onshore oil in great quantities was discovered in the early Sixties in the Sheikhdom of Abu Dhabi. The oil was located in the Bu Hasa and Habshan areas – on the edge of the Liwa sands. The Headquarters for this new operation was at Tarif and a squadron of the Trucial Oman Scouts was stationed at Mirfa with direct responsibilities concerning oilfield security.

The Ruler of Abu Dhabi at that time was Sheikh Shakhbut bin Sultan al Nahyan who could be classified as an original of the Bedu Sheikhs – a really splendid man who had little or no experience of the then modern world. The oil revenues were pouring into the coffers in Abu Dhabi and in spite of serious advice from many sources, Shakhbut deposited all or part of the money in boxes in his fort. The advice he was given was that hospitals, roads, schools and a modern infrastructure for the country must be planned and put into place.

After much argument and discussion, it was put to Shakhbut that the oil revenues should be placed into the banks – one of the main reasons was that the rodents in the palace storeroom were eating their way through considerable sums each month. There were banks on the small Corniche in Abu Dhabi at that time. Also on the Corniche were the local headquarters of two groups who were to help shape the growth of the area in the future – Spinneys and Gray Mackenzie.

With the money safely in the banks, more efforts were made to get a level of expenditure approved for the building of the nation. All Shakhbut did – according to many tales – was to visit the bank and count his money, causing much confusion.

The previous rulers of Abu Dhabi had ascended the hot seat by more foul means than fair – in that succession was normally the result of a death. The Ruling Family decided in 1966 that Shakhbut should be retired and replaced as Ruler by his younger brother, Sheikh Zayed.

Sheikh Zayed was at the time the Ruler's Representative for the Eastern Region, i.e. Governor of Al Ain. I had the pleasure, during 1966 and 1967, of meeting Sheikh Zayed from time to time – mostly when he came to Al Ain at weekends, when my squadron was based in Fort Jahili. He was a most impressive and kindly gentleman, who had the future of his people firmly fixed in focus. The development of what was to become the UAE was totally due to his leadership and direction, in conjunction with the almost magical commercial vision of the then Ruler of Dubai – Sheikh Rashid bin Said al Maktoum.

So what actually happened on August 6, 1966, which brought about this dramatic change? It had been decided that the changeover of Rulers was to be bloodless. It was not a coup in the normally accepted sense of the word. It was a carefully prepared plan with very tight control, designed to get the whole job done by midday. August 6 was perhaps the hottest and most humid day I can remember at that time.

The key players, diplomatically, in an operation of this sort were the Political Resident in the Persian Gulf, based in Bahrain, and the local Political Agent in Abu Dhabi. The Trucial States each had treaties with Britain for defence and the day to day operations were directed by Bahrein, with a British Army Headquarters, Land Forces Persian Gulf, commanded by Brigadier Holyer, with large elements of RAF at Muharraq (Bahrain) and at Sharjah, the Headquarters of the TOS.

Troops involved were 'A' Squadron (Sharjah), commanded by Major Dennis Halstead, M.B.E. (RHF), 'X' Squadron (Mirfa), commanded by Major Ken Wilson (RS), 'B' Squadron (Al Ain), commanded by Major Dennis Anstee (R.Anglian) and Support Group under the command of Captain David Neild was back up at Mafraq Crossroads. The Army operation was under the control of Colonel Freddie De Butts, Commander TOS and various RAF aircraft were used to bring troops into the area. My memories of what happened as far as 'A' Squadron was concerned are very clear. I was 2 I/C to Dennis and my tasks were pretty exacting. Quite naturally none of us in Sharjah knew what was going on – on a need-to-know basis, we youngsters were kept in the dark. Sir William Luce had retired and Archie Lamb (Political Agent) was away on leave and their deputies were responsible for carrying out the project. The Political Resident was represented by Glen Balfour Paul and the Political Agent, Abu Dhabi by Simon Nuttall.

August 5, 1966, the day before the operation, was just a normal day for the Resident Squadron in Sharjah. We were a sort of "public duties" show piece for visitors, but with an element of patrolling in the area bordering Dubai – Jebel Faiyah and the Abu Dhabi to Al Ain track. We were running a darts competition in the Mess at the time – called Mickey Mouse. The skill of the darts player is to get 3 x 1, 3 x 2, 3 x 3, etc., ending with 3 bullseyes. I do not really know how, but I had won that night's leg (August 5) and had gone to bed at about midnight somewhat tired. At about 0200 I was awoken by an orderly and had to drink several mugs of black coffee to wake up, before attending an orders group in the Majors' Compound. The whole plan was then revealed and our Squadron's tasks were then made clear to us.

I was to get to the Maqta crossing point on Abu Dhabi Island by sun up and stop travellers entering Abu Dhabi Island or leaving it. Arab officers were also involved – Lt. Hassan Said had to "neutralise" the embryo Abu Dhabi Defence Force, who were carrying out driver training on the old airstrip, with Major Tug Wilson and Captain Charles Wontner. They all returned to Barracks. 2/Lt. Salim Said had to take out and block off the telephone exchange. Dennis Halstead had to take the Armed Police Barracks next to the Ruler's Fort in Abu Dhabi by dawn and receive Sheikh Zayed by 1100 hrs. It was hoped that the changeover could be done by 1300 hrs.

The enormous humidity and oppressive heat made it difficult to take in all the briefing, but Dennis kindly mentioned that the main body of 'A' Squadron was waiting for me on the Square, ready to go. In those days the track to Abu Dhabi was about 3 miles wide, depending on the sabkha, and it took something like three to four hours to transit. The only tarmac ended on Jumeirah beach in Dubai, not far from the Chicago Beach Hotel (now Jumeirah Beach Hotel). Jebel Ali was an RAF bombing range – frequently used by Cyprus-based aircraft.

Dennis and other elements of 'A' Squadron had gone on ahead of me and I eventually made the Maqta crossing by sun up – a very bumpy and fly ridden drive – especially in the dark. There is something romantic in seeing the sun come up over the desert. I did not notice it that morning.

Abu Dhabi island was then separated from the mainland by a swampy creek and the Maqta crossing was a series of vertical 40 gallon oil drums which were filled with cement and set into the bottom of the creek, over which one drove one's vehicle. This was the only fording possibility onto the Island, and, if you look over the side of the large modern bridge today, you will see a small sentry tower which is where the crossing point was in 1966.

Not many people wanted to get in or out of Abu Dhabi on August 6th – I remember a car full of Lebanese/Palestinian businessmen in a Mercedes, which I held up for 5 hours, until I was given clearance to open the crossing. They were not pleased – there was no air conditioning in the area and they needed the petrol in the car to get to Dubai.

Years later, when I was General Manager of the Spinneys' company in Muscat, the Managing Director of the Gray Mackenzie company, Richard Owens, held a dinner party to celebrate what was I think his 50th birthday. He was describing his early days in Abu Dhabi with Gray Mackenzie at Jebel Dhanna. On the particular date that I had sealed off the island, he was going into the nearest centre of civilisation, i.e. Abu Dhabi, for one of the few long weekends available for him. He had no option but to go back to Jebel Dhanna – he never held this against me!

Eventually I left the crossing and I was directed to join Dennis in the Armed Police Barracks, where I met Sheikh Zayed. I remember him as being wonderfully calm and collected, as the negotiations went ahead. The diplomats had decided to approach Shakhbut with proposals to unify the currency in the Trucial States – this would have meant cancelling the Reserve Bank of India Rupee and discontinuing the Bahraini Dinar. A new currency was to be introduced – the QDR (Qatar Dubai Riyal), which would cover all the Trucial States.

After about an hour, the diplomats changed tack and informed Sheikh Shakhbut that the family wanted him to retire. He naturally refused and withdrew into an inner sanctum. Eventually an Arab officer, Lt. Obeid Ali from 'X' Squadron, was sent in and finally shepherded the whole family out of the fort at about 1600 hrs. I was by then at the front gate of the Fort, where I hastily put together a guard of honour, and presented arms as Shakhbut was driven to the airport, escorted by Major Tug Wilson. An RAF Pembroke then flew him over the town on his way to Bahrain, where he stayed with the Ruler, Sheikh Issa, for a short period before moving to Bushire in Iran. He was eventually invited back by Sheikh Zayed and ended his days in Al Ain.

The other Squadron tasks were achieved easily – the ADDF was neutralised and the telephone exchange ladies needed some encouragement to pull out the plugs. Salim says he fired a shot through the roof and all was done in 5 seconds.

We then set about returning to Sharjah, but Sheikh Zayed insisted that we stayed for a hafla – a great meal of goat and rice and pepsi cola, which arrived after evening prayers. We were joined by Zayed, who told stories in between sucking at his bedu pipe – a really most satisfying end to a hot, humid and very difficult day. A day that was the start of re-shaping the Trucial States into the United Arab Emirates, a model modern country.

Sheikh Zayed bin Sultan al Nahiyan

Those involved on 6th August 1966 were:

Military: Colonel Freddie de Butts Commander TOS

            Major Tim Budd   Force Intelligence Officer

Military:	Colonel Freddie de Butts	Commander TOS
	Major Tim Budd	Force Intelligence Officer
	Major Dennis Halstead	Officer Commanding 'A' Squadron
	Captain Michael Curtis	2I/C 'A' Squadron
	Lt. Hassan Said	OC 1 Troop 'A' Squadron
	2/Lt. Salim Said	OC 2 Troop 'A' Squadron
	Sergeant Ahmed Ali	I/C 3 Troop 'A' Squadron
In Support:	Major Ken Wilson	OC 'X' Squadron
	Lt. Obeid Ali	OC 1 Troop 'X' Squadron
	Captain David Neild	OC Support Group
Diplomats:	Mr. Glen Balfour Paul	Deputy Political Resident, Bahrain
	Sir William Luce (tour ended)	
	Mr. Simon Nuttall	Assistant Political Agent, Abu Dhabi
	Archie Lamb (on leave)	

N.B. There have been many different attempts over the years to make records of what actually happened on 6th August 1966. I list below the various actual locations of the squadrons, with a note of their participation on the day.

'A' Squadron, Sharjah	Major Dennis Halstead	Operational squadron
'B' Squadron, Jahili	Major Dennis Anstee	In reserve
'C' Squadron, Manama	Major Rory Cochrane-Dyet	Not involved
'D' Squadron, Masafi	Major David Severn	Not involved
'X' Squadron, Mirfa	Major Ken Wilson	Back-up Abu Dhabi airstrip
Support Group, Manama	Capt. David Neild	Back-up Abu Dhabi crossroads coffee shop

The following are the actual key points:

a. Sheikh Shakhbut was escorted out of the Palace by Lt. Obeid Ali to the Main Gate, where 'A' Squadron mounted a guard of honour.

b. Major Tug Wilson escorted Sheikh Shakhbut from the Gates to the Airstrip.

c. Much later, when 'C' Squadron was based at Jahili, they escorted Sheikh Zayed from Al Ain to take up the official mantle of Ruler in Abu Dhabi.

126

Back to Sharjah

We got back to Sharjah and during our stay as resident squadron in Sharjah, I remember that there must have been some disturbance in Arab/Israeli relations in the north. We had a slight problem at the Cola factory on the Dubai side of the creek, where rioters who wanted to go and fight in the conflict had taken to throwing bricks at American property. Dennis Halstead and Salim Said went to investigate and the rioters, confronted by a show of force from the Maktoum Bridge, plus a few shots fired over their heads, decided to go home. I think this was all started by a Bedu sitting on the end of the Sharjah runway, seeing the visiting squadron of Hunters from Akrotiri in Cyprus bomb up, take off, go and do a bombing run on Jebel Ali and come back without bombs, and this started rumours that the British Defence Forces were supporting somebody somewhere. Apparently the Ruler of Dubai, Sheikh Rashid, said that if anyone wanted to go to the Palestinian conflict he would pay for them to go, but I think the steam went out of that one very quickly.

CHAPTER 6

Roundabout again – the move to Fort Jahili

So the time came for us to go and do 'roundabout' again and, because I was suffering from a volley ball injury, Hassan Said was sent down with the advance party. Dennis drove down with the main body and I must confess it was very odd being in Sharjah without one's chums. We had thought it would be a good idea to teach the soldiers volleyball. I had learnt volleyball and the rules in 1965, when I was commanding an army youth team, where we spent our time teaching this new game, as part of the hearts and minds business of getting people to join the British Army. So we had therefore set up a pitch and started to teach the soldiers how to play this game. I had injured my knee badly and was carted off to hospital to have it seen to by Peter Swinhoe. I had ended up in a wheelchair, but not for long, and then had crutches. I remember one of those Friday morning lunch parties up at Umm al Qaiwain creek, where we had a barbeque and beer and it was autumn, so it was getting cooler. My right leg had been completely sealed in heavy polythene and I have a picture showing me lying in the sea, with this leg floating rather like a big anti-aircraft barrage balloon.

A week after the main body had gone to Al Ain, I was passed fit to travel and I had the dubious honour of going down on the Twin Pioneer aircraft.

I think a note about these twin pins (as they were called) would not go amiss here. They consisted of a flight of half a dozen of these Scottish Aviation Twin Pioneer short take-off aircraft, run by Squadron Leader Harry Bromley, and their task was to resupply and provide casevac (casualty evacuation) for the Scouts. We used to get an aircraft once a week, with the mail. All we had to do was to morse code our requirements in terms of spare parts, whisky, gin, beer and whatever else, and people going on leave or sick case medical evacuation were always taken out on these aircraft. In the main, the pilots were Polish and they were a friendly crowd.

So there I was, sitting in one of these lovely little aircraft buzzing, because there is no other word for it, across those vast tracts of desert that exist between the creek at Dubai and Buraimi. Buraimi, as it was called in those days, was a large group of oases. It consisted of about half a dozen villages, some of them were in the Sheikhdom of Abu Dhabi, hence Sheikh

Zayed's previous position as Ruler of the Eastern Region. The main village was called Al Ain, and the Omani village about two miles east of it was known as Buraimi, where the Sultan of Oman had a Wali (or mayor). Astride the border there was a very good hospital, run by Pat Kennedy, called the Kennedy Oasis Hospital. The Kennedys were missionaries from Chicago and their hospital was the very model of modern day thinking. At the time there was no border fence between Abu Dhabi and Oman and this led to some smuggling activity; for instance Toyota cars from Muscat used to go through Buraimi on their way to Yemen and no one said a word.

So the little twin pin buzzed on. Through the windscreen we were looking for Jebel Hafit, which is a very large Ayres Rock type formation, and this appeared out of the South-East after about an hour's flying. We then circled the lovely fort, known as Jahili. Here the Second in Command's job was to hold up a windspeed machine, which told the

Approach to Fort Jahili by Twin Pioneer aircraft

direction and speed of the wind, and to speak on a special radio to the pilot, who then went the three miles out to the East of the town and landed on the graded strip. That was my arrival at Buraimi in October/November 1966. The fantastic fort has been captured forever and a day in David Shepherd's painting, the original of which hung in the Officers Mess at Sharjah. When the TOS became the Union Defence Force it became the property of one of the ruling Sheikhs.

The make up of the Squadron was much the same as it was in Sharjah. Dennis Halstead was Squadron Commander, I was Second in Command, Hassan Said was the Commander of 1 Troop and Salim Said was Commander of 2 Troop and 3 Troop was commanded by a Sergeant who eventually handed over, towards the end of our time in Buraimi, to a young 2nd Lieutenant who was trained in the Jordan Officer Cadet School, called Bishr bin Bidr. He was a young Omani, who was related to the Sultan of Oman, the father of the current Sultan (Qaboos), but he came from the Musandam area. I had in this appointment a young officer of good qualities, very keen, loyal, speaking very little English, who had been trained by the Jordanian army. He brought lots of new ideas to us, but made my task a lot more difficult, purely and simply because of the language problem. He made strong efforts to learn English as we went along. The Squadron Sergeant Major, Atiq bin Murad, was still with us, providing continuity.

Fort Jahili was a large 'sugar-cake' fort about 2 miles in the sand dunes outside Al Ain and within sight of Sheikh Zayed's palace. It consisted of three sections or keeps. First of all the beautiful, round fort itself, almost Beau Geste, shining white, which was quite the most delightful of places to spend six months. If we start from the top and work down, the round room at the top, upon which was the flagpole, was the Squadron Commander's bedroom, beautifully kept, with small cool slit windows and furnished most tastefully. Outside this there was a round wall-less battlement with some outside steps leading down to yet another walled pathway round the outside of the building, which consisted of the following rooms, tacked onto the central core: first, from the stairs up from the ground floor level, was the ante room, which was part-semi-circular, nicely furnished, with curtains and carpets, that went through, with a step up, to a very nice dining room, off which was the servery. Off the servery and going round anti-clockwise was one of the Arab officer's bedrooms and going on just a little bit further was a long part-semi-circular bedroom that was mine, as Second in Command.

One came down the steps to ground level, where there was a gate through the wall to the right, through which was a long barasti (made from palm leaves) building that was divided into storerooms, the cook house and the Officers Mess orderlies' bunks. A little further on was a double-bedroomed barasti cottage, with a concrete floor, that had been built for visiting officers and their guests, and a little further on too was a double roomed elsan-type loo (we were back into the business of non-flushable loos), and to indicate the sense of humour of the various officers that had done their little piece in this neck of the woods, there was a notice, painted red on white, with a black border to it, which said

SEALED PRIVY

RESERVED FOR PRIVY SEAL,

OFFICER COMMANDING, LADIES

AND OTHER PERSONS OF QUALITY

which meant that it was the officers' lavatory! (It reminds me too of a notice of a similar sort, which I found on the edge of Dubai creek during my time there, which just said NO PISSING HERE, obviously put up by a Brit who could not write Arabic.) To the right, at the back, as one came through this door in the wall was the Squadron mosque. We had a Mutawa in each outstation, and this old chap had a really beautiful mosque, which is still there. Muslims, as is well known, pray five times a day, sometimes more, and on each occasion they have to wash. Some of my predecessors had designed and built this lovely white mosque, with its little minaret, so that the water that came from the washing place was drained off in falajes,

Guest Cottage

little channels, into a small garden, and the Mutawa was responsible for making sure that each part of the garden received some of the water.

I should say that, as a squadron, we were not responsible for the state of the buildings. The standard that had been established thoughout all outstations was totally to the credit of E.B. Wilson (Tug Wilson) of the Worcestershire Regiment, who very carefully and cunningly managed to take the best of the barasti type principle of living, in that you have a wall which let the breeze through and kept the sun out, with a concrete floor, so that, wherever one went, one had the basic elements of comfort. I was to find this not only in Jahili, in the buildings at the back, as I have just described, but also in Masafi, and later in Manama. He was a very clever chap, whose name will never be forgotten in that neck of the woods. He died in 2009.

The next part of the fort was the soldiers' keep, which was situated, as one looked north from the main building, to the right of the main gate, and consisted of a number of rooms round the inner wall, with some more rooms in the middle. Broadly speaking, this is where the soldiers slept and the keep itself had towers on each corner. The main gate was directly opposite the main fort and looking towards this gate, on the left there was the Administrative compound, within which were the Squadron Office, Squadron Commander's Office, my office, the Majlis, the arms store, the Medical Centre and small hospital, and all the other ration stores and equipment stores. Just below the main fort on the left was a small enclosed

Camel patrol, Fort Jahili

yard, which was where we parked the transport, and which was where the REME had their pit for servicing vehicles. The only other addition to the fort, just below the walls on the western side, was a small plunge pool, which I suppose was about 4 ft deep. It was in an enclosed area, covered in barasti and we could lie in that during our off-duty moments and keep cool.

We were extraordinarily lucky to be posted to Jahili at a time when it was winter. It was nevertheless hot during the day, but there was no humidity as there would have been on the coast. We had a number of jobs to do as Jahili Squadron. Our area of responsibility took in most of the land that led down the track to the Lahima airstrip, towards the Liwa hollows and the oilfields. It took us north up to Bir al Fau and Sumaini Police Post and westwards towards Abu Dhabi where we were responsible for patrolling and reporting any breakages in the water pipeline that went from the oasis to Abu Dhabi. Quite naturally, with the Sultanate of Oman nearby, we were responsible in part for watching the border of Oman, which went from the Qabil Police Post, just below Jebel Hafit, south of the fort, right the way through up to Sumaini. There was a nasty ridge of very deep sand called the Ramlet that was in the way, going North from Buraimi towards Sharjah, and we were allowed, quite openly, to go into Oman down Wadi Mahadha, through a gravel wadi all the way North, through Mahadha itself and out near Sumaini, because the shifting sands in the Ramlet made life extremely difficult and you could often get your vehicle stuck.

It was in the early part of our stay at Fort Jahili – the autumn of 1966 – that we had a visitor of some importance. Colonel Sir Hugh Boustead, who had retired from the post of Political Agent in Abu Dhabi in 1965, returned to stay at the Al Ain guest house as a guest of Sheikh Zayed. Dennis and I enjoyed his company in the oasis, which centred on riding around the villages and dinner at the fort or the guest house. He was well known in the area – most villagers recognised him and his head man, Bakri, who had worked for him for many years. To be in the presence of Sir Hugh and to listen to him talking about his life was a great experience.

We had an Intelligence Officer in the oasis, John Cousens, who was an officer from the Royal Artillery, a softly spoken fair haired, red faced fellow, who was actually a good Arabist, who got bitten by the bug of flying aeroplanes and later on he bought his own. Having got a Private Pilot's Licence, he bought a Percival Prentice, a single engined machine and flew it out from England to the Trucial States – a really most incredible

Falaj system, Al Ain

effort. He used to fly it around with Harry Bromley of the Twin Pin Squadron. Eventually, he decided to sell it and a buyer for it was found in South Africa and Harry Bromley and one of his chums flew it to South Africa to sell it for John Cousens. I remember it coming down to Buraimi, where one of my jobs as the Second in Command, was to be a sort of Airport Manager of Buraimi airstrips, of which there were three. Ours was just our side of the non-existent border, a short strip for the Twin Pins. There was what we called 'Buraimi International' which was a large, very carefully graded strip, where the surface crust had not been disturbed, which would take anything up to Dakotas and Fokker Friendships, and the Sultan of Oman's Airforce had a little one down their end near Beit Agayl, which was the Oman Gendarmerie Post, where they used to get a white Beaver aircraft about twice a week. Anyway, this aeroplane of Cousens appeared and landed all right, but because of the heat and high altitude of the place, it took three or four efforts to get it airborne. This was quite alarming, as even on the last go it only managed to clear some trees by a whisker. I think it was underpowered or affected by the heat. John lived in an Arab house in the Souq and it was his responsibility to keep us well informed about local matters.

I remember quite happy days patrolling down the Lahima track and going round the desert and meeting up with Dennis Anstee of 'B' Squadron half way between his base in Manama and ours somewhere near Bir Al Fau. When on patrol, Khan, my ever faithful orderly, would go into the nearest beduin village and buy two cockerels for curry. I would have thought that the smartest thing to do would be to cut off their heads and shove them in a cool box until the next day, but, no, he tied their legs together and tethered them to a bush close to where I was trying to sleep. They crowed all night and we ate them next day.

I remember going out on exercise from Buraimi, again towards Lahima and David Neild was an umpire. We had a collection (each Squadron had two) of long wheel based Land Rovers with a 2 litre engine, and they were known as FFR (fitted for radio) which had a 24 volt system, driving all sorts of extraordinary generators to run the radio sets. As a net result, they were underpowered and took a lot of coaxing along. In the middle of the night the one in front of me, David Neild's, broke down and there we were with a torch trying to fix it, when suddenly a voice behind us said "Salaam Alaikum". We were literally miles from anywhere, but there was a bedu with his camelstick over his shoulder and in his headdress he had got a few belongings and he was walking to Abu Dhabi from goodness knows where. Unfortunately he knew nothing about repairing Land Rovers.

I remember too quite clearly a rather disturbing incident which took place during our time at Jahili. It was never clear to the authorities why it happened, but I've got a pretty good idea and so have the Intelligence boys. Dennis had left one day, early in the morning to go up to Fujairah, to umpire an exercise which was taking place off the beaches there, with army tank landing craft that had come from Bahrein, with half a Squadron of Centurion tanks, to do an amphibious landing. Back in Jahili, something was wrong and it was difficult to pin down what it was.

I went down, as was my wont when Dennis wasn't there, from the steps of the Fort to take muster parade at 6.30 a.m. and there was nobody there. I sent for the Sergeant Major – he hadn't arrived from his home in Muweiji – he was sick. I sent for Salim Said and he came, but Hassan Said was on leave. We had what turned out to be a Squadron mutiny. Cousens was sent for and he thought he knew one part of the story, in that suddenly a lot of

135

money had been drawn out of the two banks in the oasis. We believed that one of the Sergeants had been paid to stir it up. They chose a time when Dennis was not there and I was frankly petrified. Now, I had two alternatives: sit it out and just pretend nothing had happened, in which case I would have been reneging on the dictates of military discipline; or I could get hold of a signals operator, who was still loyal, and get him to put through a message. I remember calculating how far Dennis would have gone that morning and trying to call Sumeini Police Post to see if he could turn round, but he had gone through.

I then had no alternative but to talk to Tim Budd and the Commander in Sharjah, initially by morse key and finally by voice. Khan, my orderly, proved to be enormously loyal on that day, because as the guard went off duty he noticed that they had got rifles and bandoliers. Single-handedly, he disarmed the whole lot and then little by little people appeared, swearing allegiance to myself and to Her Majesty the Queen. In the end I went into the Soldiers' Keep, sat down with a rather large pot of coffee and asked them who wanted to talk. The situation became exceedingly rough, I wasn't actually threatened physically, but they shouted and screamed and it was difficult to talk to them, so the only thing to do was to lock the door of the Keep and make sure they stayed in there.

By this time, Tim Budd and Freddie de Butts had landed by helicopter

Well water testing at Bir al Fau

and had taken up residence, so to speak, in the Majlis, the meeting room and, one by one, the various people were sent for. Word went around the oasis very quickly that there had been a slight problem. Atiq, the Sergeant Major, who had actually been ill with malaria, came in and was extremely upset to find out what had happened. He was a small man, and he darted around so much that I was afraid he might collapse, if he continued in this vein, and so I had to calm him down. The result was that a sergeant and five others, who were responsible for the mutiny, were taken away in irons, but we never knew who had paid them, and everyone was very keen to point out that there was nothing in what the soldiers had done that was in any way a reflection on my or Dennis' leadership.

Not long afterwards, Dennis went on leave and I think this was a testing period to see if I could command in his absence. So, a little under a year after my arrival as the 'reluctant scout', I was taking command of a Squadron whose morale was a bit low and whose loyalty was questionable. I think I have to thank my lucky stars for having Hassan Said and Salim Said on my side and we worked together to rebuild the Squadron. There was only one further incident that I found a little bit disturbing. 303 rounds were currency in those days and they were worth approximately a rupee each. We went to the ranges, just down by Jebel Hafit one day and, as is customary, each soldier has to give a declaration in Arabic to me, and to an Arab officer, that he had no live rounds or empty cases in his possession. Very soon, we found that there were half a dozen people who had got ammunition everywhere – they were stuffing it under the wheel arches of the Bedfords and in many other places. So I arrested the six, I collected the ammunition, we calculated how many rounds had been fired, and how many we had got left and I satisfied myself that we had in effect accounted for everything. That was the last incident, as far as I was concerned, during my time of temporary command.

The Oman Gendarmerie, on the Omani side of the oasis, was located at a place called Beit Agayl, and was commanded by a splendid chap, called Graham Vivian. We used to take it in turns to go for curry on a Friday, either to them, or they came to us. There were some characters beginning to appear in the oasis. One, whose name I forget now, worked for Balfour Beattie and he was building a road; and then another character appeared called Michael Lomas, a tall ex-Royal Engineer with glasses, ginger hair and bushy moustache, who set himself up first in the village and then in a Twynam hut. He was allegedly doing some water surveys for roads and other sort of civil engineering projects. I never really understood what he was up to – he used to go down to Abu Dhabi now and again, and once came back with a Quarter Ton Trailer for water. Some of the things he did in trying to build water towers out of Dexion were quite clearly Heath Robinson, and miles from anything that bore any resemblance to sensible engineering skills, and I must confess I had a feeling that he was some sort of intelligence spook. Another character appeared one day when I was in Jahili on my own, who said his name was Kenneth Timbrell, working for Lazards, and he had come up with Tim Budd's permission to have lunch with me and then go to see Sheikh Zayed about making investments in London. Everyone knew that the simplest way of finding Sheikh Zayed was to go to Abu Dhabi, not Al Ain, and later on, towards the end of my time in the TOS, he turned up in my life again, this time as a full-blown Colonel in command of British troops, Sharjah, so there was another one wandering around in Buraimi, with a bit of a strange story and background to him.

CHAPTER 7

The Buraimi Hunt Ball and Point to Point

In late 1966, when Dennis Halstead and I were at Jahili with 'A' Squadron of the Scouts, we decided to hold the Buraimi Hunt Ball and Point to Point. Each Squadron had its daft performances – there was the Masafi Rose Show, there was the Royal Manama week, which comprised shooting competitions and a Scrabble evening, plus a curry lunch, and above all else, the major social event of the Trucial States calendar, every year in December, was the Scouts Ball, which was held in our HQ Mess, and the local box wallas were invited. I only managed to attend two. At my first one, the Mess (we were still at Sharjah then) was converted into a beduin tent encampment, and at the second, at Al Hira, the new camp just outside Sharjah, the Mess was converted into Piccadilly Circus underground station.

Now to our Buraimi Hunt Ball, this took some considerable planning and we could only accommodate a few (about 50) to what turned out to be a complete and utter success, and really terribly amusing. What we did, Dennis and I, was to send our measurements to Moss Bros in Covent Garden and they flew out, at some quite considerable expense, two pink tail coats for us to wear as Master and Joint Master of the Buraimi Hunt. I should at this stage mention that I was still carrying on riding and Dennis encouraged this – we were allowed to use Sheikh Zayed's horses from the stable behind Fort Jahili.

The weekend took the following form: On Thursday, the invited guests, which included Pat and Jeannette Ive, the various Squadron Commanders and others arrived in time for tea in the courtyard. As the sun went down, we had the Squadron piper on top of the Fort playing a lament or whatever, and then we went off to change for dinner. We obviously needed some spare girls, so John Pitt managed to get a couple from Dubai and I managed to get a couple from Abu Dhabi and various others were found and brought in. The oil companies that had holiday villas in the wadi at the back, kindly lent us these for the weekend. So, gorgeous ladies appeared in long dresses for cocktails on the battlements, which were followed by a really superb dinner, out in the cool evening air of Buraimi. The dining room was converted into the ballroom, the ante-room was a

Colonel Pat Ive

sitting out area and there were chairs around the battlements for the young couples to sit on. We then converted the plunge pool area into the Plume of Feathers nightclub, after the small nightclub that always used to be set up for the Hampshire Hunt ball in the Guildhall in Winchester, and down there we put some cushions around the walls and beside the swimming pool, and there was a small kerosene fridge, so younger loving couples could dance, have a drink, and even swim. The night wore on and everybody enjoyed themselves enormously.

The next morning, we had some point to point races, using Sheikh Zayed's horses, with his permission. We marked out a course, with red flags, that could be seen from the top of the battlements looking south towards Jebel Hafit. One had to go round the flags from the left hand side and the course would take about 10 minutes. It was quite long and rugged, you had to jump over some laid out palm trees, and a small wadi, and it was quite exacting – not exactly like Badminton, but well laid out. The spectators were on the roof of the Fort, the girls were all beautifully turned out. It was just before breakfast, the sun was coming up, Jebel Hafit looked gorgeous with a small cloud around its crown, and off we went. We had three races. The first was the Open Race of 'A' Squadron Cup, the next was the Ladies' Race, and the final race was the Commander's Cup Race. The Open Race produced some pretty startling performances, by some officers who had never ridden in their life before. In the Ladies' Race, I remember one girl from Dubai (brought by Pitt the younger) said: "Do I have to wear a saddle?" – a comment which caused a certain amount of mirth. She wanted to ride bareback, but she fell off the minute she got on the horse, so there was one lady less for the Ladies' Race.

In the major race, we set off from the steps of the Fort and went out through the main gate of the whole complex, which could take only three horses side by side. There were 6 horses in the race, ridden by Halstead, Dinnin, Pitt, myself and a couple of others. We set off right-handed round the Fort and then headed out towards the desert. Well, within the first two hundred yards, Dennis broke a stirrup and crashed to the ground, and Dinnin and I took the lead over the others. We came to the furthest flag and I turned right. Dinnin missed this vital red flag and disappeared south like a puff of dust into the distance, in the direction of Qabil Police Post, and was not seen again for half an hour or so, when he returned very dusty and very tired. I carried on with my horse, the lovely Zuneina, and we won the race, as confirmed by the spectators from the top of the Fort.

The races over we sat down to a typical Scouts breakfast in the cool

Beating Retreat

crisp morning air, on the roof of the Fort: black velvet, mulligatawny soup, fish kedgeree, bacon and egg, coffee, toast and marmalade, paludrine tablet, brandy and this extended towards lunchtime. The guests all went home in the afternoon. It worked extremely well, it probably cost us an awful lot of money, but it was so big and so successful that there were not really any other squadron led occasions like this thereafter. Dinnin tipped up while we were having breakfast, and has accused me ever since then, jokingly, of cheating on the race, of moving or hiding the flag, which of course was not true.

CHAPTER 8

Al Ain and Mid-Tour Leave

It was during this period in Jahili that I got to know Sheikh Zayed reasonably well. He used to come up most weekends to stay in the Oasis and more often than not he would ask me to go over for coffee on the roof of his palace, and we'd sit and talk, with John Cousens, about anything and everything. He used to come up and go hawking in the desert on occasions and I remember that great big black Lincoln Continental, with desert tyres, that he drove all the way across the desert with great skill. I remember what a friendly and in fact awe-inspiring man he was. He had great presence, and when you were with him you knew he was one of the best and greatest of the Beduin Sheikhs, and this was borne out, during our stay in Jahili, when King Hussein of Jordan paid a State Visit to the Emirate of Abu Dhabi.

Part of that visit involved King Hussein flying up from Abu Dhabi to Buraimi in a Fokker Friendship, which he piloted himself. We had prepared a tour around all the villages belonging to Abu Dhabi, with graded tracks being hastily prepared, and Dennis Halstead accompanied Sheikh Zayed and King Hussein in a grey Lincoln Continental, which had been given to me two weeks beforehand to jack up and check for bombs and limpet mines. It was then guarded 24 hours a day. My task, during the visit, was fairly simple – to guard the airstrip where the Fokker Friendship was to land. We had by then got helicopters in Sharjah, once the HQ in Aden had closed, and I had a Sioux chopper under command of Mike Little, from the Royal Engineers, who was a very highly skilled chopper pilot. We flew a quarter to half a mile in front of the Royal procession round the villages, just ensuring that there were no hidden dissidents behind trees or sand dunes. A very large lunch was held at Sheikh Zayed's palace and I was fortunate enough to be able to meet King Hussein and shake his hand as he left for the airport later.

There was only one sadness at this time, and that was to do with a dog. Dennis and I had got the bug for salukis, and we had two of these dogs, which we used to race along the tracks, and they would do 28 m.p.h. To clear the Oasis of dogs for King Hussein's visit, the Municipality, such as it was in those days, had put poisoned meat down, and one of the dogs,

Pipes and drums in Al Ain high street

Dennis' bitch, picked up a bit of rotten meat somewhere near the stables. She died very quickly that day and left us with 4 puppies to hand-rear. I kept one and the other three went to the RAF at Sharjah.

We used to go into Sharjah every five weeks or so for a little bit of R & R (rest and recuperation) and I well remember on one occasion driving in (one of the two British officers went, leaving the other one behind of course) and Liz Feltham (the Deputy Commander's wife) giving me a severe ticking off for not going to see her "the minute you arrive in Sharjah". So the next time I went in, I set off at 5 in the morning, when the sand was still pretty damp from overnight dew, and drove like hell up through Wadi Mahadha to Sumeini, past the Jebel Faiyah coffee shop and arrived in Sharjah at about 6.30 in the morning. I went straight up to knock on Liz Feltham's front door and Liz, who was still in her nightie, said: "Ooh, you naughty boy, what on earth do you think you are doing?" "Liz, my love," I replied "you instructed us to come and see you the minute we came in, so here I am". "Huh," she said, "you'd better stay for breakfast". At this moment Bob Feltham appeared in his wuzra (sarong), covered in shaving

144

soap, and was not best pleased: "You're a raving madman," he said, but he allowed me to stay for a quick cup of coffee, and the point was made and talked about for years afterwards.

Back at Fort Jahili, about this time, a really splendid 2/Lt. had joined us from Officer Training, Abdullah bin Ali al Ka'abi, from the village of Mahadha, where his family had lived for many years. He was a keen, efficient officer, whom I much enjoyed having in 'A' Squadron. He took over command of 1 Troop.

Abdullah bin Ali al Ka'abi

145

Another part of the Buraimi saga to record here was the question of the border with Saudi Arabia. As I mentioned earlier, we used to patrol quite heavily down the Lahima track, which was on the edge of the Rub' al Khali and the Liwa hollows. We had to patrol it every now and then because it was an area rich in oil. The boundaries had been declared, accepted and marked by the placing of oil drums and Martin Buckmaster of the Foreign Office had negotiated the border with the local tribes. As I mentioned before, there had been an incident earlier when there had been some question as to the ownership of part of the Buraimi Oasis and the Saudis had tried to take it.

While I was at Jahili, there was an incident involving the border. The Saudis were suspected of moving the oil drums, from time to time, some way towards the Arabian Gulf coast, in an attempt to sequester land. We had to go and check on this with quite sophisticated navigation equipment. On one occasion, I remember, they had been moved and Dennis Halstead went off with the Dodge Power Wagons (which we used to have to borrow from Support Group in order to get over the deep hollows) and a couple of guides from Sheikh Zayed. We were not allowed into the Liwa without a qualified guide.

The expedition set off to attempt to get these drums put back in the right area and they had a radio, so we were in touch from Jahili most of the time. One night Dennis rang through and said they had got problems with axles, half shafts and all sorts of other bits and pieces of the Dodge Power Wagons, and that they were not far from Umm az Zumul. If you look at the map of the Trucial States, it is at the bottom right hand corner, not far from an area in the Sultanate of Oman, called Lekhwair, where there is in fact a lot of oil.

Pat Ive, who had then taken over as Commander of the Scouts, arrived in Buraimi in a twin Pioneer aircraft, full of spares for Dennis and we spoke to him and said the two of us were coming to find him. We flew down through a bit of a sand storm, and as we spoke to him, we could hear his voice getting louder and louder. We said: "We'll make for Umm az Zumul, you must meet us there". At Umm az Zumul, in the middle of the hollows, there is a very hard length of sabkha, which served as a landing strip. Of course, I had got both my cameras with me and I took photographs of the twin Pioneer on this sabkha strip, once we had landed; and then Dennis arrived, having towed one of the Dodge Power Wagons in. We re-supplied him with water, half shafts and everything else, to make sure he had what was necessary to correct this oil drum business, which took him between

Twin Pioneer Aircraft at Umm az Zumul

3 weeks to a month. This was part of the job we had to do and, at times, it was extremely uncomfortable.

Some time after this incident, Dennis went off for his leave, as I mentioned earlier, and towards the end of my time in Fort Jahili and when Dennis was still on leave, Pat Ive arrived and said to me one day that he wanted me to take over the command of the Squadron. Before going off on leave Dennis had told me that he was going to retire shortly from the British Army, but this was the first official notification that I had had. Of course I was delighted to accept the position and it just remained then for me to take over from Dennis at Masafi, which was to be our next port of call.

Before that, I too was due for some leave. This was towards the latter part of 1966, and having completed 9 months service, I was due forty-two days, so it looked as if I might be home for Christmas. The routine was to go to Sharjah and sign off. Dennis Halstead had had his leave and 'A' Squadron stayed on at Jahili until the next roundabout in early 1967.

We caught a Beverley aircraft to Bahrain. This 'maid of all work' was an aircraft that resembled a council house with wings and gave one the first impression of being quite incapable of flight. We then had to wait about two days for the chartered British United VC10 to take us to Gatwick. This involved a stay at the RAF staging post hotel, the Britannia Hotel, which was pretty grim, but served its purpose.

On the leave party were John Pitt, David Neild and Richard Dinnin. On leaving Sharjah, Tim Budd had given me a brown envelope to give to Bob

147

Brown, who was the Intelligence Officer in Salalah, who was also going on leave on the same VC10. That evening Bob appeared at the roof top bar, where I gave him the envelope. We were all there when he opened it and read it out: "Her Majesty the Queen has seen fit to award me the M.B.E. for my services in Salalah". This was a very good excuse to celebrate, which we did, without regard for the time.

We took a taxi to Muharraq airport at 20.00 hours – the VC10 was to leave at 23.59 hrs. David, John and I managed to catch the flight but unfortunately Bob did not manage to get home until Boxing Day

We were picked up at Gatwick by my father, my mother and my brother, in enough cars to get us to Kilmeston, where I had asked my Mother to lay on a 'Scouts' breakfast. David Neild's parents lived in Fareham and Richard Dinnin was going to stay with his parents on the Isle of Wight. We had black velvet, mulligatawny soup, fish kedgeree, bacon and eggs and halfway through this David Neild fell asleep and did a header into his meal, so he had to be taken out – all a matter of much mirth to my parents. Richard Dinnin, however, ("my boy" was his favourite cry) was continuing to hold his own. In the end it was up to my brother, Andrew, to drive these people down to Fareham and the station. So we went down to Fareham Creek, with Neild in the back of a mini-traveller, dropped him and his suitcase at the front door, pressed the bell and ran. Whereupon, his mother, who was Scottish, opened the window and said: "Is that him?" We said: "Yes, it is", and she said "Normal form".

We then went down to Fareham station where Richard Dinnin was going to catch a train to Portsmouth harbour to get the ferry. He looked every bit the Edwardian officer, the suitcase, the sports jacket and trousers, a brown trilby, mackintosh folded on his arm. We made sure that he caught the right train.

The leave went past very quickly and as we were not going back by chartered aircraft we had to go back via Lyneham, where an RAF Comet was going to fly us through to Bahrain. Again, we were all on it and we took off from Lyneham one wintry January morning, I seem to remember that the aircraft was grounded at Akrotiri in Cyprus for repairs, so we were put in a hotel in Limassol for two days until the spare parts caught up with us. I eventually arrived back in Buraimi with some lovely stories to tell.

CHAPTER 9

Off to Masafi, and command of 'A' Squadron

I drew the short straw and was nominated to take the advance party from Jahili to Masafi. Again this represented a totally different contrast in soldiering; whereas before in Jahili and the areas around there we had been used to the wide open places of relative peace and tranquillity, the move to Masafi was to an area that had been politically a little sensitive. There had been the odd disturbance in the area and of course there was a slight problem with the border in the north at Dibba, the border with the Oman territory in the Musandam peninsula.

I took the Staff Sergeant and his team, my orderly and my driver, the great Mohammed Ali, the fastest pair of feet on clutch and brake pedals you've ever seen in your life, and we set off north from Jahili one morning. This was a fairly leisurely drive up Wadi Mahadha to Sumeini, from Sumeini to Jebel Faiyah coffee shop, and proceeding north from Jebel Faiyah till we came onto the plain, just before the Manama complex, where we turned right up a well beaten track into Wadi Siji. After wending our way up this winding wadi we came out into a bowl in the middle of the jebel, where there were the two villages of Masafi; one on one side owed its allegiance to the Sharqiah and the Ruler of Fujairah and the one to the north owed its allegiance to Al Qassimi family, which ruled Sharjah and Ras al Khaimah. There was a very thin line between the two and right at the top end of the bowl, under the Jebel, was the Scouts camp.

The inhabitants from whom I had to take over were the men of 'B' Squadron. Richard Dinnin was now in command of this squadron, having left the Depot, and Nigel Harris was his Second in Command. Nigel had gone on to Sharjah, with his advance party. On the table of the mess, there was a stone, under which there was a note – "Problems at Dibba, boy, meet me down there with a troop". Well, I hadn't got much more than a troop with me, so I took what I had and of course the soldiers all knew the road from Masafi to Dibba. I left Staff Sergeant Nagib Ali to start the take-over of the camp and we set off down this extraordinary track, very narrow, and we got to one point, where there was a red mark on a rock face, so I asked what that was for, and they said: "Well, watch the Bedford behind". The front right hand wheel of the Bedford just bounced gently against this

Masafi Camp

red mark and in bouncing back it kicked itself just 2 degrees to the left, which enabled it to get round the very narrow bend without ripping the canopy. So we got there, and found Dinnin behind Dibba – there were three villages on the Dibba plain by the sea – Dibba al Fujeirah, Husn Dibba, which belonged to Sharjah, and Dibba-Bayah which was in Omani territory. Behind Husn Dibba, there were two marquees as a base camp, and I was told by his cook that he was on the beach.

Dinnin had risen to fame in the following way. There was a Wadi Bih, that ran up from Dibba and came out inland from Ras Al Khaimah. Dinnin had been patrolling there one day when he had come across a dhow unloading ammunition at Dibba. This was going to be taken through to the Dubai side. Dinnin arrested everyone, put them in chains and at 3 in the morning arrived down at David Robert's Political Agency Compound in Dubai, where he tied them to trees in the garden, shouted for David to issue summary justice and left them there for the Political Agent to deal with. This caused much mirth and gave Richard the reputation for toughness and fairness.

Anyway, we got down there to find a lovely old huge fort on the Omani side and there had been some problems, I think, with the rights to the fishing, or some such thing. Dinnin said: "Well now, watch this". We

150

walked up to where there were three poles in the ground and took one step over it, whereupon the fort opened fire at us. They had nothing in the fort that could have hit us, and they stopped firing the minute we stepped back a pace, but it was just a bit tantalising. The most important thing for us to do was to get Dinnin back to Masafi to do the hand-over, so I left Hassan Said to control the Trucial States villages, and make sure nothing untoward happened in the coming days. I went back up to Masafi to get Dinnin away and to await the arrival of Dennis Halstead to take over, all of which took place in a very short space of time; then everything went very quiet and that was the end of all the nastiness in that area.

Back in the Masafi bowl, the problems had been associated with water, and one lot of villagers had had a go at the other village because they were pinching all the other lot's water, and then there used to be the odd crackle of rifle fire now and again, but our presence there generally kept it quiet. The camp was enclosed in a barbed wire compound, which had about nine concrete huts down one side, then the Medical Centre and Squadron Headquarters, with the radio shack on the other side, it had the Sergeants' Mess up at one end of the square with the main cookhouse behind it and it had REME workshops all in a dirty old cluster of barasti. The Officers Mess consisted of one permanent building, which was an ante-room cum dining room with a kitchen behind it and a series of 5 marquee tents with barasti on the end, in which the officers had their rooms and sleeping

Donkey Patrol, south of Dibba

quarters – very rough indeed. Through the barbed wire fence to the edge of the wadi, there was a footpath that led to a shed with the elsan loo in it. We took over as quickly as we could and despatched Richard Dinnin and his henchmen down the track to Dubai, and then got around to cleaning the place up, realigning most of the barastis and tidying up everything else.

After about two or three weeks of life in Masafi, Dennis retired and left. I was very sorry to see him go. Contrary to all expectation, I had managed to get on with him extremely well. A lot of other people thought he was a wild Scotsman and rather difficult, but I found him exactly the opposite. He'd been in the Royal Scots Fusiliers with David Niven and Brigadier Charles Dunbar in Malta. So, he came from a first class regiment, had got an M.B.E. along the way and, as far as I am concerned, he was a very good soldier.

On Dennis' retirement, I took command of 'A' Squadron, which had come through a mutiny and had come through a 'roundabout' without any problems. It had acquitted itself well in its 'fit for role' tests and I had Hassan now as my Second in Command, with Abdulla bin Ali, Salim Said and Bishr bin Bidr as troop leaders. Now at this point, I want to bring in another player into the mix and his name was Robert Shields, known as 'the walad' (Arabic for boy), who had joined us at Jahili, after a spell with 'D' Squadron. I came across Robert at the Abu Dhabi coffee shop one day when I was driving from Abu Dhabi to Buraimi. He was a young Second Lieutenant, who had been commissioned into the REME and had got a year or so to kill before going up to Cambridge and, as his father had been a senior officer in the REME, he'd got him onto a short attachment to the Scouts. He was the only British 2nd Lieutenant in most of our time in Masafi. He was a very nice chap indeed, who had taught himself Arabic. He gained invaluable experience in soft skin vehicles in desert terrain, which was to set him in good stead when he went back to the REME.

Robert also saw first hand vehicle trials of the new forward control long wheel based Land Rover, which we had in Masafi for some considerable time, undergoing tests. A funny thing on that model was that the steering track rods on the front are long and cumbersome, and we hit a rock with this new vehicle and damaged one. The Rover technicians who were sitting in the back, with lots of clocks, dials and paperwork, were all terribly worked up about this, and Rashid bin Subayha, who was the Squadron Commander's driver took one look at it and said: "Well, sidi, are they going to sit here looking at it all day, or do I repair it?". So I replied: "Let's just find out and I asked them: "Well, what are we going to do?" They said "We haven't got a spare and there's no spare in Sharjah". So I said to Rashid: "Repair it." He undid it at both ends, took it off, beat it straight with a couple of rocks and put it on again. Not only was Robert Shields absolutely astounded at what had happened, but so were the Rover technicians. Anyway, we got home after that, with no problems.

Robert then went off for a short time to do a vehicle study on a new recovery vehicle, and carried out trials between a Berliet, a Scammell and an Antar, and he spent a lot of time dragging stuff through the jebels to see which was the best. I think the Berliet came out well. He was at Masafi for a short time and was a very useful bloke to have around, if only to stop me going barmy.

I suppose at this time I was working too hard and I probably wasn't taking enough notice of my own health, not eating enough fresh fruit and vegetables, and I went down with a bad case of prickly heat. Prickly heat is a particularly nasty rash, which is caused by sweating profusely, and the pores of your skin getting blocked with salt. There are one or two old wives' stories about how to get rid of it, like standing in the pouring rain, or anointing yourself with Johnson's Prickly Heat powder. I found it extremely difficult to wear a shirt so, in the end, Tim Budd, who had come up in one of the helicopters said: "I think you had better have a long weekend off". Hassan took command and I went down to Sharjah, where I had four or five days of decent sleep in air conditioning, good food, not too much booze, and went back at the end of it, thoroughly refreshed. I suppose these things do happen, but it's just a warning that not only has one got to be careful about people and things, but you also have to take care of yourself and eat properly.

Masafi was, as I said, the principal place to ensure that there were no problems between the Sharqiah and the Qassimis. There was also another problem that was looming in those days and that was one of illegal immigrants. They used to come across from Baluchistan, from Jawani and Gwadur, and land anywhere on the coast between Khor Kalba and Husn Dibba, trying to avoid entry procedures and to catch lorries to Dubai. We would have to try and round them up and sort them out. It really did get beyond the pale, and at one stage I had to move the whole of my Squadron from Masafi. I also had half 'X' Squadron from Manama and one troop from David Neild's Support Group. We lined the cliffs from north of Khor Fakkan almost all the way to Fujairah. Less emphasis was placed on the

Illegal immigrants in Khor Fakkan

Northern sector, as there were no roads there and steep impenetrable mountains. We then had the Force dhow, which was known as Al Qaid, permanently in Khor Fakkan with its crew, and 0.5 inch machine gun mounted on the bow. We had a Royal Navy minesweeper and two sorties a day of RAF Shackletons from Sharjah, and with all this put together, I co-ordinated the anti-illegal immigrant patrols on that coast for about a month and a half. This was when the wind was in the right direction and they thought they could come in without diesel engines. These dhows used to hold anything up to 150 people and they had all paid considerable sums to come to Dubai, where the streets were considered to be 'paved with gold'.

The practical application was simple. Dhows were met at sea and escorted to Khor Fakkan. The Captains (or nakhodas) were sent to Dubai, where they were taken to court and fined. In the meantime, the passengers were placed in a secure barbed wire compound, with the remaining crew members. The Wali of Khor Fakkan was responsible for providing food and water during the period. On the Captain's return, the dhow, with passengers, was escorted to open water, with strict instructions not to return.

I also had at this time a helicopter. As I explained in the Jahili chapter, now that the Aden conflict had finished, the helicopter squadron came up to Sharjah, and three weeks out of four, I had a small Sioux helicopter.

They used to take it in turns to come up and live with the Squadron. One time it was Hugh Lovett, from the Queen's Own Hussars, a charming young officer, who drove with great skill and when we were coming back from the coast, we used to stop and fill up one stretcher with water melons and one with fish and fly straight up the Siji and back to Masafi, where we lived like lords. Then I had two Sergeants – one was called Sergeant Jackson from the Parachute Regiment and another young Sergeant called Courtney.

We used to do active patrolling with the Squadron troops and go up the coast from Khor Fakkan through Fujairah to Khor Kalba to Khatmat Malaha, where the border with Oman was situated, and another patrol used to go up and down the inside of the jebel, south of Manama, on some occasions, without getting the Squadron at Manama too fed up. When this was all going on, I was able to see the whole of my patch in a day, with the chopper, instead of every three weeks, by Land Rover and donkey patrol. I used to go out and spend the day with the patrol – the chopper used to pick me up somewhere else and take me back, and so on.

At this stage of my life with the Scouts, another character appeared and this was Captain Jim Stockdale, from the Royal Hampshire Regiment (my Regiment), who had last served with the battalion at Lemgo in West Germany in 1959 and had gone to the Scouts, where he had learned Arabic and took a very vital part in the intelligence gathering network. He was

Khor Fakkan from Chopper Zulu 81

the I.O. on the Batinah coast, as that coast was called, and he used to live with me up at Masafi in the hot weather. He was very good at chess and he used to beat me. He never drank, except orange juice. For his work, in the Trucial States, he was awarded the M.B.E. sometime towards the late 1960s. He didn't give up then, but went and did a further tour as an Intelligence Officer with the Sultan's Armed Forces in Oman.

It was a hectic time in Masafi, I'll make no bones about it. One day, for example, I had been rushing round checking on my patrols, when a Bedu came in and started beating my desk with his stick. We got a quick translation: there was some bloke sitting at a well at Khatmat Malaha, with boxes of rifles and ammo. So we got a quick half-Squadron and took half a day to get there (my chopper was being serviced, so we couldn't use that). We went down there, and sure enough, there was this bloke with light brown hair and blue eyes, wearing a shamagh and agal, but not in any known recognised way. I spoke to him in Arabic and he didn't say a word, so I hit him with a camel stick and he swore at me in English. "Right", I said, "I think I've got the measure of you. Who are you and what are you doing here?" He didn't say anything. So I said: "Right, you're under arrest", shoved him in a Bedford with all his boxes, and took him back to Masafi. There I did an Oscar, Oscar (classification of a very urgent message) to Tim Budd, saying I had found this creature; and I got a message back, which said quite simply: "Put him back." I sent him back down there, but I never really knew what that was all about, whether we were taking some arms across to the Sultan or whatever. There was a character who lived in Sohar in those days, called Carl Seaton-Brown, whose only great hobby was shooting grouse, and I had on previous occasions to take through a Bedford load of shotgun cartridges to him, but I don't think this was connected to his shooting. However I didn't ask any questions.

Another day, I got another Oscar, Oscar message from Tim Budd, who was Force Intelligence Officer, which said: "The village of Kalba is arming itself, will you please go and sort it out". So I went down overnight, put pickets round the village, and we sent somebody in. The next thing I knew, two helicopters were clattering down – one had Bob Feltham in it and the other one had Tim Budd in it. They all rushed into the village and came back very red-faced later, Tim Budd saying: "Yes, well my spies down there had said that something was going on, but there's some bloke there who is cleaning a Martini Henry rifle and it's all got out of context". So we all went home.

Later on, somewhere near Fujairah one morning, there was a fight between two factions over a garden, and I thought it best to go and sort it out. I told Sharjah what was happening, and Jim Stockdale, and off I went. These two factions were looking at each other about two hundred yards apart, and there was a very prosperous garden, with a little Lister diesel pump in it, on the well. There was some dispute as to whose well it was and whose water, and all the normal nonsense. I drove down the middle, parked my Land Rover, got the coffee beans out, started roasting them, then grinding them with pestle and mortar, and making coffee, and then I said to one chap: "Go up there and get their boss" and to another: "You go up the other side and fetch their boss". They all came down, very friendly, and I said: What's upsetting my day down here is you lot firing at each other", and then they started swearing about whose garden, whose well it was; and this was the only time that I brought out the Martin Buckmaster map and said: "Right, do you agree with Buckmaster?" They all said: "Yes", so I said to one side: "Well then, Buckmaster says that this garden belongs to you" and to the other side: "Why are you making the fuss?"; "Ah, but the well is mine". I said "No, no, no, the well belongs to whoever's land it is on, and it's all logged with the Government". So they all went away, and we counted up the empty rounds, because it was important to collect them, otherwise they had a nasty habit of reusing them. I think we collected something like 1,500 empty cases and they had been firing for two days. There had only been one injury – one man had been hit by a rock

Landing from Force Dhow after coastal patrol

splinter and that was the only blood that was spilt in that particular incident.

Not long after this, I went off on the Force Dhow and patrolled from Husn Dibba to Kalba. Again we were looking to see if we had tidied up the illegal immigrant problem properly. This expedition nearly ended in disaster, because when we were down near Kalba, one of those sudden storms blew up and we had no option, as the sun was going down over the jebel, but to try to get into Kalba. The only way we could do it successfully was to throw an anchor out on a very long rope and go in stern first to the shelter of this rather difficult creek. We just kept the engine running all night and held onto the rope off the bows. I must confess that I was very glad when I got back to Khor Fakkan and got into my very hot Land Rover.

Weekends here were difficult for a bloke who was on his own. By this time, Robert Shields had left, Hassan Said used to go to Sharjah on a Thursday to see his family, the other Arab officers used to take off and I used to get left on my own. The simple solution to all this was that down at the bottom of Wadi Siji was the Depot, the Resident Rifle Squadron in

Rain at Masafi

158

Manama and the Support Group, and there were always one or two chaps around there, who I could go and have lunch with, and I must confess that they were all very good about this.

There was Leslie Barron, who commanded the Training Depot, who had David Goodchild, on loan from the Sultan's Armed Forces at the time, as his Second in Command. He was the chap I'd shared a bedroom with in Aden, learning Arabic many months before, and he was a musical Welshman, who played the harp. There was David Neild and his bunch of thugs in Support Group, and Ken Wilson commanded 'X' Squadron, which was in the Rifle Squadron Lines. 'X' Squadron was a little bit of a 'panache' squadron and if you went to breakfast with Ken Wilson, all you got offered was "a puff of fresh air and a paludrine tablet". Ken didn't eat very often – he was a thin, wiry little Scotsman, who was very popular. His Squadron had the doubtful pleasure of having more Dhofaris in it than most and his rise to fame was that he called his Dhofaris his 'Jocks'.

The Dhofar problem blew up again during my time at Masafi, because it became 'leave time', in that the time was right for the dhows to go to Salalah on the coast of Dhofar. There was a very simple formula that was worked out about leave. Force Headquarters had issued instructions that no more than x% of your Squadron was to be on leave at any one time – a fairly sensible and realistic instruction. Out of that percentage, a certain number were allowed to be Dhofaris, and when they went on leave, they went on long leave, which was two or three months at the end of their two and a half years, and as I said before, if they didn't come back, then we reckoned we had had our money's worth.

Very simply, I got hold of my 'king' Dhofari, who was a Corporal in one of the rifle troops, a first class chap, very level headed, and I said: "Okay, we're coming up to Dhofar leave time. According to instructions issued to me by the Commander, Col. Pat Ive, this is how many can go". So we looked at the numbers and we looked at who was due to go on leave, and there were two who were not due for leave, but who wanted to go on leave, for some dubious reason. So I said: "Well, as far as I am concerned, that is what is allowed and that is what is going to happen". The next thing I had was two Dhofaris going round, raising absolute hell, morning, noon and night on this, and I must confess that I was very glad when Pat Ive came through with somebody on their way to see the Ruler of Fujairah, and stopped off for coffee with me. I said: "Would you like to adjudicate a quick problem", and it was all sorted out. All those who were due leave went, and those who were not eligible did not go until the following year. They all understood it, they all knew it was the law, they all knew that the Qaid had said so and that it was Queen Elizabeth's wishes. That was the end of it.

On one occasion I had spent Friday at the Depot and we had had a very good lunch with Leslie Barron and then the sky went black and I said: "Hullo, there is a flash storm in the jebel and these things can be pretty nasty". I had heard about John Pitt, when he was Acting Paymaster, and going to Jahili with the pay wagon, having his windscreen broken by hailstones as big as golf balls, when he got caught in a flash storm. All the money, which was in a box bolted to the floor of his Land Rover, got soaking wet in the flood and it took him 3 days extra on the pay run because he had to dry the money out. So I thought: "Well, I'd better have a go for it, before the rain actually starts to fall". The main road in Wadi Siji went up the floor of the wadi and I remember going round one corner (I had a pretty new Rover is those days – 53 EN 53 – and the heavy wax protection was still on most of the engine – to this day I thank God that it was) and a couple of hundred yards in front of me was a great big wall of brown water, about 10 ft. high. Quick as a flash, I shot up a side wadi, as high as I could go and scrambled up the side of the wadi to watch this lot go by. The Land Rover was awash, but it didn't get sucked away, thank goodness, and when the water went down, I drove up to Masafi and found that most of the barasti and tents in our camp had been blown away, and such blokes as were there at the weekend did a very good job in sorting it all out.

My time at Masafi went pretty quickly – I was very happy. I had a good Squadron. They all respected me. They saw that I enjoyed what I was doing. While on leave in England, I had gone to the Aldershot stores, and bought a pace stick, upon which I had placed a small brass name tag, and had given it to wee Atiq, my Sergeant Major. I used to stand there at muster parade in the morning, and he used to be going up and down the lines – you couldn't see him because he was so small, but you could hear him barking and shouting, like a little Jack Russell in a field of corn. He was very meticulous and we used to have a proper muster parade every morning. I remember one day Brigadier Charles Dunbar tipped up as Director of Infantry and he took the muster parade and was very impressed by Atiq's efficiency.

Only one other incident is worthy of note: one morning we jumped into the chopper heading towards Dibba and the rule was that we'd climb to so many thousand feet and then we'd radio Sharjah, something like this: "Hullo, Sharjah, this is chopper Zulu eight one, we are airborne Masafi, bound for Husn Dibba. Time of this flight probably 2 hours. We will radio return to Masafi." They used to reply: "Chopper Zulu eight one, this is Sharjah, we hear you, Roger and out." Then we got up high, and we were just heading down one of the finger wadis off the main branch that went off to Dibba, when RAF Sharjah came up and said: "All aircraft operating south of Dubai, be warned that there are 6 Hunters operating." So I looked at the pilot and he said: "South of Dubai, they're obviously going down to Jebel Ali bombing range." This was a long way from us and in a different direction so we assumed we had nothing to worry about. Just as we got to the mouth of this particular wadi, these Hunters went past us, just 150 ft. in front of our nose. The turbulence, of course, caused the chopper to fly in a most unstable fashion, to the point where the pilot, and I think it was Sergeant Jackson, had to wrestle with the controls to stop it turning over. So I said: "Get me up higher, and I called up Sharjah and said: "Listen, your stupidity nearly killed me. If you mean 6 Hunters operating south of Dibba say so, but you said Dubai. I'm reporting this matter now to the Commander of the Trucial Oman Scouts, and I think you had better just have your log book ready when he gets down there." So I switched to a new frequency and got hold of Pat Ive and told him what had happened and he asked: "How are you?" and I said: "Shaken to bits". I said: "It really is so stupid when this sort of thing happens". Anyway, the air traffic controller was given a hearty telling off.

By this time I had got myself quite a reputation for being a gourmet cook. What I used to do to attract people up at weekends was to go and shoot some sand grouse down on the gravel plain, near the little airstrip of Tayyiba and shoot a couple for each person coming. We used to have a starter, then these sand grouse as main course, and the pudding was normally cling peaches cooked in a frying pan with some brandy, which was a novel way of doing things. I remember Bob and Liz Feltham used to come up quite a lot and David Roberts, Political Agent, Dubai, who had sadly lost his first wife, used to come up with his nanny and the children and spend a weekend with me. All these were very happy days, with very nice people, and I had a fair lot of visitors.

CHAPTER 10

The move from Masafi to Manama

My last days with 'A' Squadron and return to Sharjah before going home

Roundabout came round again and we bundled up and hadn't got far to go this time. Our next port of call was Manama, literally down the Wadi Siji, turn right and two minutes you were there; into a big military conglomerate, where the most important thing was to be seen to be smart (as the complex was closer to Sharjah and therefore visitors), smarter and better than all the others in everything that we did. So we took over the Infantry Squadron lines, sorted all that lot out and I began to realise that my time was beginning to come to an end.

I had arrived in the Trucial States in April 1966, it was now December 1967 and I was due home in early 1968. I handed over 'A' Squadron, with a very heavy heart, to John Whitelaw, who had eventually managed to extricate himself from the G3's office and become an infanteer again. He didn't like what he found in my Squadron and was very difficult during the handover, in particular with the ammunition box count, as some of lead seals were broken and he thought the boxes might be full of stones, not

Manama Camp

ammunition. What had happened was that when we went out onto a range, before you could stop them, the Jundis (soldiers) kicked open the lead seals on all the boxes to hand out the ammo for shooting practice, and at the end of the range period, we filled up the boxes with the right amount of ammunition, but we did not have a new replacement lead seal. So John radioed Pat Ive and said Curtis was short of ammunition and a Board of Officers was convened. Then, while I sat in the Mess drinking coffee, they counted every round and found that I was actually half a box over the top for some reason. The handover went relatively smoothly after this.

Prior to the handover, something very odd had happened. I had had an Adeni signaller and we had two 31 sets which we used as manpacks, as well as 88s. One of them went missing and we never ever found it. To be able to use it, someone would have had to take the other one as well, but we believe it may have been stolen by this Adeni signaller. A Board of Enquiry took place under David Morris, but there was no conclusion and little fat Ali, the Signals Corporal, was mortified by the whole thing.

So, one morning, I went out and took my last Muster Parade, and as I handed over to John, the Squadron suddenly grounded arms and they lined the road from the Officers Mess out of the front gate and some way down the track that led to Sharjah. I was very moved, I had my orderly with me, and my faithful driver and standing on an oil barrel at the gate, rigidly at attention and saluting, was wee Atiq, my Squadron Sergeant Major. As we slowed down beside him, I put my arms out, whipped him off the oil drum and popped him on the seat beside me in the Land Rover

My Farewell

and made as if to make off with him. It was a very moving time, that morning, and I think it goes to show that perhaps I had the right idea where they were concerned. They knew that I was a strict, but fair infantry officer, they knew that I tried hard to do the damnedest I could for them in all situations and they trusted me. All very odd when you think of the circumstances under which I went there in the first place, as a reluctant Scout.

Down at Sharjah, all that remained was to hand in the kit and be dined out. By this time, the Headquarters of the Trucial Oman Scouts had left the camp in Qassimiah and had now moved to Al Hira, just between Sharjah and Ajman, to a purpose built camp. This move was so that the British troops could have a presence in the Gulf for desert training, in the old camp, next to the RAF. I had won a 50 rupee prize for designing the front gates of this new camp and that was where I was dined out one night with John Pitt and lo and behold, at the table, opposite me, was this fellow Kenneth Timbrell, in the full regalia of a Colonel in the Blues & Royals. Having told him that we had met before at Jahili, I was then kicked under the table by Pat Ive and I let bygones be bygones and we had a really first class meal. I think Colonel Timbrell had been on a look/see visit to the Trucial States, on the earlier occasion, before establishing British Troops Sharjah, which he commanded.

New camp at Al Hira

I think it was one of the first times that girls were allowed into dinner and we had Jeanette, Pat's wife, and Liz Feltham and maybe one other. After dinner, we went out onto the balcony where there were two brass cannons, which had been made by the apprentices' school, many years before. One was called COMTOS and the other was called COMTESSA and the trick at dinner nights was to put a lit thunder flash down the barrel and to stuff it full of potatoes very quickly. This we did, firing at each other across this small patio. The next thing we noticed was a cannon firing back at us from the little town of Ajman, not far away, and it was then, with complete horror, that we realised that by firing cannons, we had signified that someone had seen the moon and that Ramadan, the month of fasting, was about to start that year. Hastily, emissaries were sent to the various Sheikhs in Ajman to explain that this was not the case, so a disaster was averted.

It was a very good dinner night and a very sad performance when we caught a Beverley and flew to Bahrain to wait for the RAF VC10 to take us back to Lyneham. My father and mother picked me up there and took me home to Gastons, where I had 112 days leave before joining the Royal Hampshire Regiment at Netheravon, after an absence of something like three or four years. That is another story, but to finish it off, having got back to Salisbury Plain soldiering, which is really very boring, and having been accused by the Commanding Officer of losing a no. 2 cooking burner, I felt the time had come to either leave the army, get married, or go back to the Scouts. So I wrote to Pat Ive and said: "Enough is enough of this nonsense, I wish to come back". He promptly offered me 'A' Squadron back again — I still have the letter to prove it — when John Whitelaw left. I formed up in front of the Commanding Officer, a man called Sandy Wilson, and said: "Sir, I wish to resign, I want to go back to the Trucial Oman Scouts", and lo and behold, he said I was far too important as 2IC of 'B' Company to go back on secondment, so there we have an ironic conclusion to the whole story. The reason why I was sent in the first place was because of an administrative muddle. I had not volunteered, I had no desire to be sent all the way out there and to go through all the horrors of Aden and learning the Arabic language. In the end, going back after the mid-tour leave, I realised that I really loved the life out in the TOS, because there was a definite job to do and one that I could do well. I had moved from reluctant Scout to committed Scout, but unfortunately that had come to an end because now the Army needed me elsewhere.

165

CHAPTER 11

The Final Chapter

What effect my time with the Trucial Oman Scouts had on my future working life – a brief history

I left the army in 1972 – there had been the threat of an amalgamation of my regiment with the Gloucestershire Regiment that happily never happened. My regiment was reduced to one company (the Minden Company) for a time, and the rest of us were posted to the Glosters, first in Heathfield Camp, Honiton and then in Minden, West Germany. I stayed with them for about nine months, during which period I trained 150 drivers for the tracked APC (armoured personnel carrier) vehicle, and was O/C Command Company, before being demobbed in April, 1972.

I had spent much time searching for a job and finally accepted a post at Boots the Chemists in their Middle East department. After a year in Nottingham being trained, I was sent to Beirut with my family. My wife and young daughter took to the wonderful atmosphere of Lebanon very well and we enjoyed the lifestyle there before the start of the civil war. My job (number 2 in the Regional Office) involved a lot of travel around the Middle East, and my knowledge of Arabic and local customs helped my work enormously. We were repatriated from Lebanon in the autumn of 1975 owing to the problems of the civil war, and having been promoted to Regional Manager, I was tasked with finding a new base to keep the business going. Amman, Jordan was chosen as the Regional Office and we lived there for four and a half years, first working for Boots, and latterly for a French pharmaceutical group, Clin Midy. Amman was much quieter than Beirut, commercially, but very enjoyable from the point of view of my family, now increased to three children – two daughters and a son.

Unfortunately, Clin Midy was taken over and I was made redundant. We had to return to England and I found a job as General Manager, Rockware Plastics at Reading and we lived in Winchester. The company needed drastic restructuring and had been rather lacking in leadership, but in time I achieved a 10% increase in sales and a 7.5% increase in net operating profit. I enjoyed the challenge of making the company profitable, but missed the travelling and the international life, so I decided to join a

Lebanese group that was trying to build a business that would be ready to launch when the Lebanese civil war was over. It was exciting work collecting up all the abandoned agencies, but the war did not end soon enough and I found myself looking for another job, aged 45.

Happily I joined Spinneys, the major food agency, catering and supermarket chain in the Gulf, and I started as number 2 in Dubai. I had not been there a year when the Managing Director (a jovial ex-Gurkha) offered me the Muscat branch as General Manager. I moved there in 1987 and there followed seven years of re-building a large company, which operated six supermarkets, controlled the biggest food/grocery group in the Sultanate and fed 7,500 people a day in the oil fields. On top of this we supplied 36 warships and 16 tanker aircraft in the first Gulf War in 1990–91. When I reached 55 in 1994, my contract ended and I retired.

I then had a period in Sharjah and Dubai, working on a series of marketing projects for the Ruler of Sharjah's nephew, Sheikh Salem bin Mohammed al Qassimi, who required me to sort out his wholesale food and tobacco operation, and then followed two years as Consultant and General Manager for the Safestway supermarket chain, owned by Sheikh Faisal bin Sultan al Qassimi, who is chairman of the GIBCA group of companies. My task was to return the chain to profitability, and having identified the main problem and submitted a report on these to the Board, my job was completed and I returned home.

Here I established a consultancy group called MEDEA – Middle East Direct Export Assistance. This was made up of a team of businessmen who had experience not only in the various Middle East markets, but in product groups as well. For example, if any enquiries for food, drink or pharmaceuticals came up in markets that I had known, then I would take them on. Tony, my co-author, worked on items which came up for consideration in Saudi Arabia and the Levant. In Gulf markets we were helped by a business contact, who did most of the in-market research. In other markets, we were somewhat hampered by the reluctance of clients to cover travelling costs. The idea was good in conception and we had some success, but it came to a natural end.

I have many happy memories of my time in the Trucial Oman Scouts. As I have said: "It is an ill wind," and I hope I have explained in enough detail how my knowledge of the Arab world and the Arabs had such an effect on me and was responsible for the various successes that I achieved. The really ghastly bit was Aden, both from the school angle and the riots and shootings.

The Arabs were kindness itself – welcoming, polite, helpful and in an

Army context very loyal, with few exceptions. If you were fair, patient and understood their problems, meted out decisions in a calm manner and handled them with patience and sympathy, they respected you for it. At times it was almost too difficult to choose which troop to take tea with after the evening call to prayer. It was always a joyful session full of reminiscences and laughter. A happy squadron could always be heard singing in the back of their vehicles for miles around. The true Bedu always concocted up a nickname once he had got used to you. I had several, depending which collection of soldiers I was with.

There were some very competent officers who served in the Scouts. I think I was very lucky to have served under Freddie de Butts, even though he did not like the fact that I was not a volunteer. Before he left I felt that he had come to terms with all this and accepted me. Pat Ive was every Scouts' favourite commander. He had the patience of Job and many other good qualities that endeared him to everyone. There were of course many others, but these two played a great part in calming down my initial anger and impatience at being the scapegoat for some incompetent staff work.

'A' Squadron had had a very successful history as an independent unit. At Jebel Akhdar they had performed well in all roles and those who were left did not hold back the information about how Captain Peter Chambers MC of my regiment had died of wounds in that conflict. At midnight on 22 December 1971 the Trucial Oman Scouts ceased to exist and they became the backbone of the Union Defence Force of their country.

If you have sincere Arab friends, they will never desert you. I have had two years in and out of hospital, fighting cancer. My squadron sergeant major, Atiq Murad al Abdulla, who lives with his family in Al Ain, was always ringing up to find out if I was still alive – I will never forget it.

Appendices
Part One

Appendix 'A'

Rulers and Senior Sheikhs in the Trucial States and Oman in 1959–61

Muscat and Oman		Sultan Sa'id bin Taimur
The Omani Bani Ka'ab tribe		Sheikh Abdulla bin Salim al Ka'abi
Abu Dhabi	Ruler	Sheikh Shakhbut bin Sultan
Ruler's representative in the Al Ain/Buraimi area		Sheikh Zayed bin Sultan
Dubai	Ruler	Sheikh Rashid bin Sa'id
Sharjah	Ruler	Sheikh Saqr bin Sultan
Ajman	Ruler	Sheikh Rashid bin Humaid
Umm al Quwain	Ruler	Sheikh Ahmad bin Rashid
Ras al Khaimah	Ruler	Sheikh Saqr bin Muhammad
Fujairah	Ruler	Sheikh Muhammad bin Hamad

Appendix 'B'

Officers who served in the Trucial Oman Scouts in 1959–61

Lt Col AEG Addison   Royal Scots

Maj PS Allfree   East Surrey Regt

Brig DW Anderson CBE   Royal Highland Fusiliers

Capt MStC Baddeley   Somerset and Cornwall Light Infantry

Col DJC Bannister MBE MC   Devon and Dorset Regt

Col HJ Bartholomew OBE   Kings Own Border Regt

Col MLA Baugniet   Royal Army Service Corps

Maj PM Baxter   Devon and Dorset Regt

Maj VW Beckhurst MC   Royal Army Pay Corps

Lt Col JPS Bidgood   Royal Electrical and Mechanical Engineers

Col TJ Bowen MC   Worcestershire Regt

Maj M Budd MBE   Royal Artillery

Maj WA Bullard   Cameronians

Brig CWG Bullocke OBE   Devon and Dorset Regt

Capt PV Burnand   14th/20th Hussars

Maj RFW Burnett   Sherwood Foresters

Maj E Carson   Kings Regt

Col SLA Carter OBE MC   Sherwood Foresters

Lt Col SAR Cawston   Royal Artillery

Maj GA Charrington   9th/12th Royal Lancers

Maj PF Chubb   Royal Fusiliers

Brig NH Cocking   Royal Tank Regt

Maj DJ Cosgrove   Kings Regt

Maj IM Craig-Adams   East Surrey Regt

Capt CW Criddle   Somerset Light Infantry

Col DL de Beaujeu OBE   14th/20th Hussars

Maj FX de Vivenot   Royal Artillery

Capt JO Fisher   Royal Signals

Capt DE Foulds   Royal Artillery

Maj JP Gouriet   15th/19th Hussars

Lt Col RGM Green MC   Sherwood Foresters

Maj JFH Gregory   Staffordshire Regiment

Lt Col JBJ Halford   Royal Signals

Maj NA Hallidie   The Green Howards

Maj CC Hammick   Grenadier Guards

Maj GA Harford   Royal Artillery

Maj SJA Hargrove   13th/18th Hussars

Lt Col EH Hillyard   Royal Army Medical Corps

Maj ERL Jones Royal Welsh Fusiliers

Maj AHB King   Kings Regt

Maj AH Laing   Royal Tank Regt

Lt Col JS Landau   Royal Artillery

Major BS Lee   Royal Anglian Regt

Maj CWT Lumby   Royal Anglian Regt

Maj AC Mason   Royal Green Jackets

Brig AWM McKinnon OBE   Royal Signals

Lt Col DL Merrylees   Royal Corps of Transport

Capt DEG Neild   Kings Regt

Lt Col MD Parsons MBE   The Loyals

Maj WJB Peat   Royal Anglian Regt

Maj RJL Pott MBE MC   Kings Own Border Regt

Maj RL Pyle   Royal Army Medical Corps

Capt H Roden   Royal Army Service Corps

Lt Col AJ Rundell OBE   16th/5th Lancers

Maj JG Savage   Royal Artillery

Maj RJ Sewell   Royal Electrical and Mechanical Engineers

Maj GA Shepherd CMG   Royal Tank Regt

Lt R Sibbick   Border Regiment

Maj BRC Smith   Royal Inniskilling Fusiliers

Maj WH Stevens   Duke of Cornwall's Light Infantry

Maj WF Stockdale MBE   Royal Hampshire Regt

Col OB Taylor   Royal Army Education Corps

Maj MF Timmis   17th/21st Lancers

Lt Col ME Vining   Royal Inniskilling Fusiliers

Lt Col AB Wallerstein   Royal Tank Regt

Maj RLG Weir   Royal Army Service Corps

Maj K Wilson MBE   Royal Scots

Brig CW Woodburn   Royal Engineers

Capt DNS Woodruffe   Staffordshire Regt

Part Two

Appendix A

Trucial Oman Scouts
Order of Battle 1966–67

	1966	1967
Commander	F.M. de Butts	K.C.P. Ive
Deputy Commander	R.H.B. Feltham	R.H.B. Feltham
D.Q.	D. Glazebrook	C.J. Adami
S. Capt.	J.K. Pitt	J.K. Pitt
G2	R.L. Shotter	R.L. Shotter
G3	R.J.G. Whitelaw	R.J.G. Whitelaw
FI0	M. Budd	M. Budd
G3 Int.		S. Theobalds
OC HQ Sqn.	R.J.L. Pott	B.S. Burns
2 I/C HQ Sqn	Mul. Midfa	Mul. Midfa
Paymaster	D. Tibby	R.T. Bedford
Quartermaster	K. Armitage	D.G. Williams
OC S & T	R.C. Wallace	A.R. Parkin
2 I/C S & T	S.W. Swindells	S.W. Swindells
OC REME	G.S.C. Cornish	J.K. Langdale
2 I/C REME	C.J. Squires	C.J. Squires
OC Signals	J.D. Morris	H.R. Williams

170

2 I/C Signals	I.J. Crouch	J.R. Potier
OC RAMC	P. Swinhoe	P. Swinhoe
2 I/C RAMC	M. Fitzgerald	M. Fitzgerald
Dentist	A. Young	A. Young
Boys School	D. Dykins	D. Dykins
OC Depot	R.H.H. Dinnin	L.N. Barron
2 I/C Depot	Mohd. Saleh	D. Goodchild
DIO Ras Al Khaimah	A. Ffrench-Blake	A. Ffrench-Blake
DIO Batinah	W.F. Stockdale	W.F. Stockdale
DIO Buraimi	J. Cousens	J. Cousens
DIO Abu Dhabi	G. Gowlett	G. Gowlett
DIO Sharjah	E.B. Taylor	E.B. Taylor
HQ Int. Staf		D. Henchman
		P. Prescott
OC 'A' Squadron	J.D. Halstead	J.M. Curtis
2 I/C 'A' Sqn.	J.M. Curtis	Hassan Said
OC 'B' Sqn.	D.G.M. Anstee	R.H.H. Dinnin
2I/C 'B' Sqn.	Faisal Bin S Al Qassimi	N.D.J. Harris
OC 'C' Sqn.	B.S. Burns	R.S.Cochrane-Dyet
2 I/C 'C' Sqn	Abdulaziz Bin M Al Qassimi	J.A.N. Devereux
OC 'D' Sqn.	A.P.P. Ricketts	D.B. Severn
2 I/C 'D' Sqn.	R.C. Pitman	L. Wilkes
OC 'X' Sqn.	K. Wilson	K. Wilson
2 I/C 'X' Sqn.	M. McClellan	A. de P. Gauvain
OC Sp. Gp.	D.E.G. Neild	D.E.G. Neild
Temporarily attached to 'D' & 'A' Squadrons in 1967		R. Shields REME

Appendix B

Salim Said

The story of Salim is the story of a young, intelligent Dhofari, who had been brought up in Salalah, in the south of Oman. Salalah, the main town of the poor deprived area of Dhofar, is where the Sultan of Muscat and Oman, as it was known in those days, chose to spend most of his time. I have met Salim's father, who in his own right was a wealthy man, and despite having the name of Al Said, was not of the ruling dynasty, though I suspect was not too far removed from it. So Salim, in those days, in the early to mid sixties, decided that he was going to become a

soldier, and felt that the best place to get his training was with the British. He came across, like lots of others, to Sharjah, where he was very quickly identified as officer material and was sent, after spending some basic training time, to Mons Officer Cadet School.

On his return, he joined 'A' Squadron in Sharjah when we were Resident Squadron, which was where I first met him. He was a very quick thinking lad, powerfully built and extremely loyal and reliable. Dennis and I could trust him to carry out any task that he was given and he always did it to the best of his ability. His troop, no. 2 troop, was his pride and joy and he trained it, nurtured it and brought it up to a very high standard of military skills. It was always a great pleasure to see him with his two Bedfords doing the various drills, and after due time, as proficiently as the Light Troop, no. 1 troop, under Hassan Said, who had four Land Rovers. The competitive spirit between Hassan, who was of Trucial States coast/Baluch origin and Salem from Salalah was very keen. The third troop was left out of this competition, but we were to get another young officer for this troop towards the end of our stay in Jahili. Salim acquitted himself well in all the patrolling we did when we got to Jahili, and was a most useful member of my team. He continued to work for us diligently in Masafi, and later in Manama and was recommended by me, before I left, to undergo further training. The next step up the line for him was the Machine Gun course at Manama, which he attended after I had left the Scouts.

He came back and joined Support Group, which in my time had been under the command of David Neild. David had all the Dodge Power wagons that existed in the force and had a Browning machine gun troop, a Headquarters troop and a 3-inch mortar troop. I think David had done some support platoon work before his service in the TOS as he had certainly had a wide and varied military career. Support Group was subsequently under the command of Miles Stockwell, an officer from the Royal Welch Fusiliers.

I was not around at the time, so I cannot tell this next story from my own experience. I only know what Salim has chosen to tell me himself, what Dennis Halstead told me later and what other people have told me. All the stories match up. Salim went on leave. The Dhofaris were allowed to go on leave, as I explained

before, sometime after two and a half to three years and I think, in the case of officers, if they had proved their loyalty, they could go a little earlier. There were aircraft in those days, particularly RAF aircraft, flying down to Salalah regularly as this area was in the grip of what was known as the Dhofar problem, an insurrection against the Sultan, led by insurgents from Aden. I am not going to talk much about the Dhofar war, because it was a long, complex and drawn-out affair, and there are many books and stories which explain in great detail how the Sultan's Armed Forces defended themselves against the Aden-led Communist guerrillas, going under the guise of the Popular Front for the Liberation of the Oman and Arabian Gulf. Suffice it to say, they did not win the war. With British officers and help with training, and help from Iran, the insurrection was finally put down, after some considerable time.

It is said that Salim, having arrived back in Dhofar on leave, was forced to join the Communists, because they had taken various members of his family hostage. There are other stories that say that he went over the border on his own accord, with the promise of great wealth. Whatever the truth of the matter, he was classified as absent without leave from the TOS, and the insurgents put him in charge of the Chinese 81mm mortars that fired regularly at Thumrait and Salalah. Salim denies having been to Peking to learn how to operate them, but it is said that he was very effective in their use. There are people who will tell you that when Salim was sober he could drop mortar bombs on a sixpence and that would cause a lot of problems in the Omani lines of defence. When he was not sober the bombs went everywhere. Salim told me many years later, when he wanted to talk about it, that the Communists used to herd up the hill people and put them in caves and say, "Now pray to your God for food". They would keep them starving for a time and then produce food from the Communists, not from God. The people were thoroughly demoralised by the Communist propaganda.

Towards the end of the war, His Majesty Sultan Qaboos issued a decree that all those who wished to return to Dhofar could do so. There was to be an amnesty provided the insurgents came across with a Kalashnikov. One day, the story has it, a very thin emaciated young man, or what was purported to be a young man, gave himself up somewhere in the Salalah region with a rifle. He said who he was, nobody believed him and he was kept under lock and key. He was suffering from dysentery, various other illnesses and lice and was in a very bad way.

At this time Dennis Halstead was serving in the Oman Gendarmerie. He had left the Scouts and had gone home to try his hand at running a riding stable, found that this was not profitable and had joined the Qatar Defence Force, under the 'mad Mahdi', an Englishman called Cochrane, turned Muslim. Dennis had not found this to his liking and had moved to Oman to join the Oman Gendarmerie, a border police force. He was stationed in Khasab in the part of Oman that is at the top of the Arabian peninsula and, as he was the only person who could identify Salim, he went down to Salalah to see Salim. He told me that he was taken to this cell and there crouched on a small stool in the corner was this dreadfully shabby relic of human nature. When he saw Dennis, he burst into tears and without any further ado Dennis said: "Yes, this is my Salim". Salim has also told me this story and also that he then spent nearly a year in hospital, recovering from his illnesses.

When I first visited Muscat as a civilian in 1972/3, I stayed at the hotel which was to

become the Falaj Hotel and I went to have lunch with Dennis Halstead at Seeb where he was then stationed and he told me this story.

Salim recovered and quite naturally, as he says himself, he felt the need to repay the debt to the Oman, and he joined the R & D (Research & Development) Ministry, which later became known as ISS. He did this in the rank of Major, I believe, and then, when he retired, he took a job in the Ministry of Regional Muncipalities. I had not seen him for years and years until I went to Muscat in late 1986 as a full-blown box wallah (civilian businessman) to take charge of Matrah Cold Stores. A very dear friend who had been in the Scouts with me, Nigel Harris, was already working in Muscat for a local company called Tawoos. One day he bumped into Salim, literally, in the Souq and gave me his phone number. So with a certain amount of trepidation, I rang this number and a familiar voice answered it in Arabic. I said "Salim" and he said "yes" and I said "It's Mike Curtis" and there was a long silence and that deep booming laugh that epitomises Salim came down the phone and, after asking me where I was, he said "I'm coming to see you". I remember at that time sitting in my office in Ruwi, and a very large, jovial, jolly, rotund, clean-shaven Dhofari, comes into my office and falls on my shoulder. We sat and drank coffee, in the old time-honoured fashion and told each other what we had done since I had left the Scouts towards the end of 1967, and what he had done, which I have tried to tell, I hope as faithfully and truthfully as I can, in this chapter.

Salim came to see me one day with his dear old father, who was visiting Muscat. I suppose he had come to see the Sultan. He came into my office in the full regalia of an elder of a Dhofari family. He had a little beduin pipe, we gave him coffee and he spoke to Salim in the unique Jebali language, which I did not understand at all. He smoked his little pipe and every time he had finished it, he tapped it out on the side of his chair and scattered ash all over my carpet. He also cleared his throat a number of times, alarmingly, but without dire consequences. Over the years that I had been in Muscat I was privileged to be invited to dinner at the Medina Club on the hill behind Madinat Qaboos, which is where the officers of ISS have their club, and I often bumped into Salim there. He used to ring me every now and then for a chat and about twice a year he would come to see me.

He had many English friends, one of whom was Ted Taylor, who was a British Army Officer from the Queen's Regiment. He was a linguist and he got a very good M.B.E. for working for Britsmix in E. Germany. He came to the Trucial Oman Scouts towards the end of my time, as Desert Intelligence Officer, and he went on to do one or two other jobs in the same vein, before leaving the army and coming to Muscat in the mid/late 80s, when I was there, to work for W.J. Towell. He was then the link with Salim, if we wanted to see him. Salim came to dinner once or twice at my house and graced our table with his presence and stories and booming laughter, always impeccably turned out in his Omani headdress and dishdasha. He was always very respectful towards my wife and grown up children and I look upon him as a dear and earnest friend.

I last saw Salim early in 1993 in the car park of my supermarket at Medinat Qaboos in an almost brand new Toyota Landcruiser with his wife and three or four of the prettiest girls you could wish to see, all beautifully turned out, all chattering away.

I stopped and chatted to him for some ten minutes, upsetting the traffic trying to get in and out of the car park, but as his car had government plates, nobody made a fuss. He made a promise to come and see me again, as he always did, but he had been promoted in the Ministry of Rural Municipalities and his duties kept him mostly out of town. In spite of his earlier desertion, he is now a very loyal member of His Majesty Sultan Qaboos's government and it is people like him who have done so much to help the development of Oman.

I feel very privileged to have made so many Arab friends, because friendships of this sort are, I think, rare in the Arab world. One does not necessarily have the same sort of friendships that one experiences at home with old schoolfriends or fellow officers, but if you have a friend who is Arab and you respect each other, then you have a friend for life. I expect that if I returned to Oman and walked down Ruwi High Street, I might bump into Salim and we could pick up our friendship again quickly. Other very good friends were Atiq bin Murad, my Sergeant Major, who retired as a high ranking officer in the Abu Dhabi navy and now lives in Al Ain, and Sergeant Abdullah Gadayah, who ended up as a Colonel and Defence Attache for the U.A.E. in Khartoum, and who I also saw when I visited Al Ain. When I look upon my friendship with these people which was gained purely and simply through respect for me as their Squadron Commander (latterly), I like to think perhaps that even though I had not wanted to go to the Trucial Oman Scouts, I have possibly contributed, through these friendships, a little bit towards the goodwill that exists between my country and the Arab world.

Appendix C

Characters along the way

Nigel Harris

I first met Nigel Harris on the Teuterberg in West Germany sometime in 1962/3. He was with the Queen's Surreys at Oxford Barracks in Munster and we (the Royal Hampshires) were in Waterloo Barracks. They were the enemy, I think, on some exercise we were doing and I remember this red-faced fellow, wearing plus fours and a hat with a feather in it, accompanied by a couple of little farm urchins, wandering into the laager we had set up with our Humber pigs (armoured vehicles) and screaming abuse in German, taking down number plates – he was obviously acting as the farmer who was going to claim off the Control Commission for damage that we had done. We discovered who he was later, when he threw a thunderflash at Bill Reeve-Tucker's pig. From then on we had instant parties in each other's messes in Munster and this was the beginning of our long friendship.

My next job was in recruiting in Hampshire, following the death of a fellow officer, Colin Winchester, who was tragically killed when his pig rolled on him. Lo and behold, Nigel then came to do the recruiting job at Guildford, so I saw more of him there, on the borders of Hampshire and Surrey. Then I told him that I was going off to the Middle East and he said: "My goodness, that sounds awful". So, off I went one way, off he went another way to join his battalion in West Germany and the next thing that happened was that I got a postcard: "Dear Michael, I am coming to join the Scouts. I hope you don't mind. Love Nigel". He came as second in command of 'B' Squadron. I met Gay, who was to become his wife, there too, when

Nigel brought her to see me in Buraimi. There was a dramatic incident – she dived into the little plunge pool, knocked herself out on the bottom and had to be rescued.

After my time in the Scouts, I went to Netheravon, had a six months spell in Cyprus with the United Nations, got married, had a tour in Northern Ireland, did public duties in London, then back to Germany before leaving the army and joining Boots the Chemists in their Middle East office. We were posted to Beirut and had lived there for about a year when a postcard arrived: "Dear Michael, I am coming to Beirut to go to Shemlan to learn Arabic. I hope you don't mind. Love Nigel". He arrived to stay, having travelled overland from England, driving a banned motor car in the form of a Ford Cortina (Fords were black-listed in the Arab world at that time), with Gay and two children, Simon and Sarah, and went to live on the hill above Beirut at MECAS, the Arabic school (Middle East Centre for Arab Studies), at Shemlan. He was there to do a course with a view to his doing an Arabic speaking job in the Army, but for some extraordinary reason he was never sent anywhere in the army to use his Arabic, so he resigned his commission and went to work first in England and then for the Dubai Defence Force.

I used to see a lot of him in Dubai as I went there often on business, having a large area to look after for Boots. I then left Beirut because of the civil war and set up my office in Jordan, running the whole of the Boots Middle East operation from there, and Nigel appeared again, now working for the Dubai Transport Company, which had some connections with Jordan. I moved out of Jordan and back to England, where I saw him once or twice on leave, than the next thing that happened was that I sent him a postcard: "Dear Nigel, I am coming to Dubai to join Spinneys. I hope you don't mind. Love Michael" and I moved into Dubai in 1986. He obviously thought this was too much, and after a few months told me that he was going down to Muscat to work for a company down there, which had got better prospects than the dry docks (the company he was working for) in Dubai. So off he went and two days later I was able to ring him to say "Guess what?" and he said: "What?" and I replied: "I'm coming to Muscat too". I had been promoted in Spinneys and went to Muscat as General Manager of their company there, Matrah Cold Stores. We lived in Oman for seven and a half years. During that time I was invited to say a few words for their daughter at her wedding to Andrew Clark at Saltwood Castle in Kent and it gave me great pleasure to recall that Nigel and I had soldiered together for the best part of 30 years, both in uniform and out, and that I remembered Sarah from her days in nappies. The Harrises stayed in Muscat several more years after we had left, and then moved to France, where we have had many happy visits. Sadly Nigel died of cancer in 2009.

Dennis Halstead

As I mentioned earlier in the story, I think the last time I saw Dennis was in the early 1970s, when he collected me from the Falaj Hotel in Muscat and took me down to the Oman Gendarmerie Mess at Seeb for lunch. Dennis was a truly wonderful person, who was devoted to his wife and family and did his utmost for them. He had left the TOS to go home to set up a small riding establishment, with stables at a place near Oswestry in Shropshire, where he had been on the staff at some stage at the Junior Leaders Battalion. His wife, Jean, was the epitome of a really sound Scottish lady and she was the power behind the throne. While Dennis had gone off and earned all the money, she had looked after the family, put together all the nuts and bolts of the riding school, arranged the weekend residential courses, fed the students, took them to stations and things like that. She was a great person and did a wonderful job there, but for Dennis, the call of the hot, wide, open spaces was too much for him and he had returned to work in the Arab world, first in the Qatar Defence Force, then in the Oman Gendarmerie and then as a camp boss for a construction company in Saudi Arabia. This he did extremely well.

I remember visiting Dennis and Jean at Hinford Grange with Rachel a few months after we got married in May 1969. We stayed there for a few days to see them and to ride some horses across the Welsh hills and that really opened my eyes to what Dennis was trying to do at his riding school. Everything was going particularly well, when the phone rang in the middle of the night and it was the Royal Hampshires saying that we were going to Belfast in two days and would I return to the camp. So our visit was curtailed and that was our last visit to Hinford.

It was a great sadness to me to hear that Dennis had died of cancer, having come home on leave from Saudi Arabia. When he arrived in England, obviously not well, the considered opinion of the airport doctors was that he should go straight to hospital. He refused to do this and his daughters, who met him at London airport, drove him straight up to Shropshire because he wanted to see Hinford. They drove through the night and they put him in a chair on the terrace at Hinford, where after a day of looking over all that he loved so much, he died and he is buried at Whittington. Jean, of course, at that stage was left with three daughters, Sarah, Susan and little Fuffy. Jean sold up everything in Shropshire and moved to London eventually to be near her girls and took a small flat somewhere near Wimbledon. For four or five years she was the administrator, in Putney, at a house for gentleladies of Scottish ancestry, a job which she did with great vigour and enthusiasm. In 1992 she sadly died of a heart attack, was cremated and buried next to Dennis in Whittington in Shropshire.

Pat Kennedy and his hospital at Buraimi
This was across the wadi, more or less on the border, on the road that led from Al Ain village towards Hafit, and it was a collection of hastily built houses made of breeze blocks and barasti. It was run through Christian missionary funding from America. There was no other hospital in the Oasis at the time, though there was the odd local government doctor. I remember once, when we had been out to have a meal somewhere, I suddenly became extremely ill with stomach cramps and practically passed out. Dennis was perfectly all right, luckily, and he whipped me into Kennedy's Oasis Hospital, where Pat looked at me and stretched me out on the table. I thought: "Here we go, he's going to do something". I was given a quick shot and I had a stomach pump. A day later, I came to after it all and it took me a good week to get my spirits back.

Pat Kennedy was a truly devoted man. He had his wife and a few American doctors, of one sort or another, assisted him in providing medical care in this emerging area in the mid 1960s. He did an enormous amount of good work, in going round the villages in the area, even in Oman I believe, tending the sick and looking after the various problems, such a child birth, death, and so on. The fact that it was a Christian missionary hospital never seemed to worry anybody. The fact that medical facilities

were being provided was of great benefit and I am quite sure that the government of Abu Dhabi at the time realised this. It was only in later years that the government went all out and built a whole series of hospitals right across the length and breadth of the Sheikhdom.

The Felthams
I had first met Bob and Liz Feltham in Munster in 1964. He had been cross-posted from the Devon & Dorset Regiment. He had been in the Parachute Regiment too and he was the very epitome of a very good heavy infantry officer. He was the Second in Command of the Cheshires. They were in the next door barracks to us in Munster and we obviously saw a lot of them. Liz, his wife, was very jovial, with a smashing sense of humour, and a really good regimental wife. For some extraordinary reason and I suppose one can only put it down to the vagaries of different regiments, the Cheshires did not like having someone from outside as the second in command. Bob only did one tour there and he disappeared after the Cheshires had been to Cyprus on U.N. duty. Imagine my surprise, as I mentioned earlier in this story, when I found him Second in Command, or Deputy Commander, of the Trucial Oman Scouts, on that rather hot day in April 1966. Of course he recognised me and, from the stories I have already told, it is clear that they looked after and became almost an uncle and aunt to all us youngsters, and they were always extremely hospitable, very kind and really a most essential part of life at that time.

We all left and went our ways at the end of 1967/68. After I had left the Army and joined Boots, I re-found Bob Feltham, believe it or not, as a Lieut-Colonel, doing a tour of duty with the Kuwait Liaison Team in Kuwait, and they had a lovely house down on the beach, not far from the Hilton

Hotel. So, every time I visited Kuwait, I either had a meal with Desmond and Hennie Cosgrove, who were up there with KLT, doing some job or other, or with Liz and Bob in their lovely house. It was always very nice to see them up there and to take a meal off them. I remember once I was up there and Bob had some extraordinarily hefty pain in his stomach and was carted off to hospital and subsequently had to have part of his stomach removed, from which he, with the true grit of a Devon and Dorset, recovered and actually stayed on in Kuwait as a contract officer for some years after that.

They retired to their cottage in Herefordshire, where we saw them last, and every Christmas one of the first cards we ever get is a wee ditty from Liz. I always remember her saying: "Ooh, hoo, hoo, you really are a naughty boy, Michael". Bob sadly died when we were in Oman and Liz died in June 2010.

Abdulla bin Ali al Kaabi

Abdulla bin Ali al Kaabi joined 'A' Squadron as one of the young officers while I was at Buraimi. He had been at the Depot, I think, for some time as a training subaltern, and he had been to Mons Officer Cadet School and he was a Queen's Commissioned Officer. He was a really thoroughly likeable, knowledgeable and keen young officer. Abdulla was very impatient to get on. He came from the area of Mahadha and Buraimi and I remember once stopping off to see his old father in the village of Mahadha. Abdulla, short, handsome, with a black moustache, always impeccably turned out, and with a very keen sense of humour, became one of the real pit props of 'A' Squadron over the years, under me and later under John Whitelaw. He took over the Light Troop when Hassan Said took over as Second in Command in Masafi. Abdulla left the TOS

in the late 60s to join the Abu Dhabi Defence Force. I do not know much about his career with them, but he did well and retired in the rank of Major General, having been Chief of Staff of the Abu Dhabi Land Forces. I have spoken to him once on the phone since then in London, and Atiq, my ex-Sergeant Major, sees him from time to time. So, here is a most important person, who was a good Platoon Commander, who obviously benefitted greatly from the training that he received in England and with the TOS to rise to such heights in the army of his country.

Hassan Said

Hassan Said reached the rank of Lieutenant Colonel in the Abu Dhabi Defence Force (Logistics) and has retired to Sharjah. When later I retired and worked in Sharjah I used to take tea with him in his office. He runs a small estate agency business. His younger brother, Juma, reached the rank of Brigadier in the Abu Dhabi Defence Force.

David Goodchild and his Welsh harp

Readers may recall me mentioning a quiet Welshman from the South Wales Borderers, a chap called David Goodchild, with whom I had shared a room in Aden, learning Arabic. He had gone into the Sultan's Armed Forces as an Intelligence Officer, but after a certain period in Oman, and certainly within my two years in the Scouts, he had been seriously ill with malaria, or hepatitis, and had come out of the desert to be Second in Command at the Depot in Manama under Leslie Barron. I remember going down to one of these jovial evenings that they had down there, and it was being held in the Infantry Squadron Mess and David had come across with his harp. This harp had been everywhere with him. I do not recall it in Aden, but it had been sent on in his luggage to Muscat, transferred to the Trucial States with him and here it was in the Mess at Manama, and after dinner he was going to play a tune for us. I saw much more of David later on when I had left the army, joined Spinneys and went to Muscat, where I found him as one of the contract officers in charge of adventure training, teaching young Omanis canoeing, orienteering, mountaineering and all that sort of thing. He still had his beloved harp with him.

He came from Bedgellert in Snowdonia, where his widowed father lived in the family home and had a twin brother who worked in the City, I believe. It is rumoured that his father taught the Prince of Wales how to speak Welsh. David used this house quite naturally as his home and his base for his many travels around the world, which included going to his father's houseboat on the lake at Srinagar. There had been a fire at his family home and he had lost all his possessions, military memorabilia, etc. I know how he must have felt, because I am literally cluttered up with stuff from my life, which I am loath to throw away, but to have lost everything in a fire in one's house is pretty shocking. However, the harp was not involved and at this particular point of time, in Manama, in 1967, there was this concert he gave after dinner. He played the harp extremely well. One drunken lout, who shall be nameless, after the performance, knocked the harp off the dining room table and it hit the floor, breaking along every seam and join, coming apart in a pile of what could only described as nasty looking metal wire. Naturally, David was more than upset, he was devastated, in fact there were tears in the poor chap's eyes, as we picked up the pieces, and I believe it cost him an awful lot of money to have it repaired.

In later years, when he was in Muscat again with the Sultan's Armed Forces, there was a man called Chris McNeely, who was employed to look after the instruments used by the various bands of the Sultan's armed forces, and one of his favourite tasks was to make sure that the harp was kept in good order. When David left Oman we were invited to dinner to the Headquarters Mess at MAM (Muasker al Murtafi'a – the Army camp near Seeb) and afterwards he was to play the harp as a farewell concert. Regrettably, half way through, something went wrong, and the noise became not unlike a dying cat, and I think some of the joints had become loose again, and the wires had become out of tune. He left Muscat to return to Wales, with his beloved harp, and sadly we have not seen him since then. He was a very nice, tall, fair-haired Welshman, very straight and honest and a very nice chap to have known.

Other Scouts – Where are they now?

There are a number of old Scouts who get together fairly regularly at the TOS lunch every year in London. This is organised by the Trucial Oman Scouts Association, which was set up by Leslie Barron and is now run by Graham Barnett.

I was one of the very few people that actually did time at all the TOS outstations in the Trucial States before Humhum Camp (a new camp at Ras al Khaimah) was set up. I think I have mentioned most of the officers who were there at the time: Freddie De Butts, Bob Feltham, David Glazebrook, John Pitt, David Neild, Nigel Harris, Richard Dinnin, Ray Shotter, John Whitelaw, George Cornish, Keith Langdale, Tim Budd, Richard Wallace, Tony Parkin, Simon Swindells, Derek Dykins who ran the boys school, Dennis Anstee, Rory Cochrane-Dyet, Tony Ricketts.

As I said, John Pitt was Director of Sports and Leisure Activities for the Borough of Wandsworth, Desmond Cosgrove was in the Protocol Office in the Ministry of Defence. Richard Dinnin remained in and around Arabia, after his service with the TOS, as Personnel Manager for Shell, then Savrola, a company making cooking oil in Saudi Arabia, then Spinneys and ending up with Airwork in Bournemouth. He married Jenny, whom he met while he was in the TOS and has two daughters, one of whom lives in Dubai. John Whitelaw runs his own little company and trots around the Middle East selling freezer equipment and lockable security post boxes, and acts as agent for various financial companies. David Neild went on from Support Group to command B Squadron for a short time and then he went to start up the Sharjah National Guard, where I saw him in the early 70s. He then moved on from that to start up the Ras al Khaimah Mobile Force. When he left the Gulf, he went to Kenya with the aim of being a Safari tour leader and I next saw him in Beirut, staying at the British Club, where we had a couple of beers to discuss a book he wished to write about his time in the Gulf. He later moved to Rhodesia, and then retired to South Africa, where he plays a lot of golf.

Appendix D

A look at what it was like 20 years ago

This paper was written when I was number two in Spinneys, Dubai in 1986. I had moved out unaccompanied to join this great group as services manager under Philip d'Abo, an experienced hand in the expatriate scene.

This paper compares the Emirates 1986 with the Trucial States 1966.

It had been on a hot dusty afternoon in early 1966 that I had stepped from an RAF Argosy at Sharjah airport. I had arrived from Aden to take up an appointment with the Trucial Oman Scouts – much against my will – as I had been due to go with my regiment to the Borneo confrontation. I had reluctantly done 3 months in Aden learning Arabic and soon learnt that I was to be Second in Command of 'A' Squadron based at that time at Mirfa in far west near Jebel Dhanna.

The nickname 'reluctant scout' was soon pinned on me and happily the others soon forgot it. At that time there was little oil about – ADPC (Abu Dhabi Petroleum Company) and ADMA (Abu Dhabi Marine Areas for offshore oil) were emerging but there were a couple of Spinneys shops. There were no roads, except a few in Dubai and the Jumeirah Beach Road which stopped with a 15 foot drop somewhere near Chicago Beach. The clock tower was all by itself on the way to the airport and the Maktoum Bridge had not been open long, but with a single span. It was a toll bridge, but TOS vehicles were exempt.

I was 26 years old, unmarried and had spent nearly all my military life in UK, Germany and a quick 2 years in the West Indies. The country where I now stood seemed like the end of the earth. All seven Sheikhdoms were emerging into the 20th century, some with ease and some with difficulty. Our job was to police the whole area and to provide peace and stability, so that the political and economic development could take place. There were eruptions and inter-tribal fracas, all of which were breathtaking at the time, but very amusing later. Can you imagine a mob stoning the soft drinks factory by the Strand Cinema? It happened and we had to sort it out.

I was lucky enough to be one of the few British officers to be stationed in all the Scouts outstations. The birth of the Abu Dhabi Defence Force meant that by 1968, Buraimi and Mirfa were not in our area. We were never allowed into the Liwa unless Sheikh Zayed had given his permission and only with one of his guides. Today it is a bit like the New Forest, with people in 4-wheel drive vehicles everywhere.

We had a force dhow, Al Qaid, which must have been one of the fastest around. We used this for patrols against gun runners and illegal immigrants on the east coast. The phenomenal growth since the late sixties has brought the area into the 20th century with a bang. The withdrawal of British troops, the birth of the UAE (initially without Ras Al Khaimah) and the very rapid development of oil, leading to the building of roads and ports, hotels, office blocks has put a completely different face on the place.

In 1966 I used to drive into Abu Dhabi once a month from Al Ain to do the shopping for the two British officers in our squadron, always with Spinneys. The manager, an immense character called Hugh Freeland, lived with Sally, his wife, in a wooden cottage on stilts outside his cold store. This was not far from where the Al Ain Palace Hotel stands today. I used to stay a night or two and head back with my Land Rover loaded with tinned goods and a small freezer box (very new in those days) with some frozen steaks as a treat. Look at Abu Dhabi today in comparison. It is just incredible how it has developed. In Dubai,

there used to be one Spinneys shop in Al Nasr Square, by the Cable and Wireless office, but I do not think the Jumeirah shop had opened by then. Hassani's, another local supermarket group, was well established by 1966.

Sharjah in those days was the centre of our universe and it had a big Spinneys which supplied the TOS and RAF Sharjah. It was run by a young Lebanese chap called David Eid, who was always very helpful. Sharjah today is much smaller and less prosperous than Dubai, whereas it was the more important place in 1966. Its importance declined due to the silting up of Sharjah creek and the consequent reduction of dhow traffic. However, it now has a very fine big new souq and there has been a great emphasis placed on the restoration of old houses and the souq area and the setting up of museums.

Going back to Dubai to work for Spinneys in 1986, the first free moment I got I drove up to see what was left of the Scouts' buildings and camps. I have mentioned before that the Scouts moved out of the main camp in Sharjah and moved to Al Hira, where I designed the front gates and won 50 rupees for my trouble, and there is still part of the UAE Defence Force up there (it was originally called the Yarmuk Brigade, after the Scouts were disbanded).

The old camp where I joined the TOS is now no longer. The square is still there, but all the buildings have been knocked down, from the RAF gate right the way through to the square. You could see that parts of some of the buildings on the crest line have been taken over by Etisalat (the UAE communications company), because there are some dish aerials and storerooms. You could still see the ruins of the Commander's and Deputy Commander's houses. On the Cavalry Lines, on the North side, where we used to have a squadron of cavalry, the buildings are there, but all the roofs have been ripped off and it's just a pile of rubble.

So I set off to try and find the old graveyard and I knew roughly where it was. I parked my car and I walked through some scrub and I found it, totally desecrated. The gravestones, which were the standard Ministry of Defence type, had been smashed. The lettering on the graves had worn with age, there were some Christian Indians, some of whom had died of car crashes, and their names were still decipherable, in the graveyard too. Somewhere in there, as I said before, was the grave of Don Tibby. It was all very sad. I went down to see Jack Briggs, because Sheikh Rashid of Dubai had given an area in Jumeira for a Christian churchyard and suggested: "Could we not either get some money to redo the churchyard, or get the remains put together and taken to Jumeira and have one simple stone, which says: Here lie the remains of the following people from Sharjah". But Jack was very realistic. He had seen this all happening over the years and he said: "There's no point in trying to redo the churchyard, because obviously the Muslim youngsters will go and beat hell out of it", so it was decided to leave it. However I can report that when we left the U.A.E. for the U.K. in 1993 the churchyard had been repaired and stones replaced, including one for Don Tibby. The graveyard was restored again and re-inaugurated early in 2010.

To summarise my time in the Scouts, the most striking memory I have concerns the people. They were always very polite and helpful, and looked upon us as the final arbiter in any argument. The country folk, mostly Bedouin, loved to argue and talk for hours on end about almost anything. They had a wonderful sense of humour and seemed to be able to drag something amusing out of anything. Distances in

those days were terrific, if only in the mind. It used to take four to five hours to go from Dubai to Abu Dhabi and much the same from Abu Dhabi to Al Ain. It took the best part of a day to go from Sharjah to Mirfa (Jebel Dhanna). From Al Ain to Dubai/Sharjah, via the Ramlat and Sumaini was five hours, depending on the sand. Today this sort of memory disappears fast as you go to Abu Dhabi in under two hours. The old Jebel Faiyah coffee shop, which was an oasis of tepid pepsi in 1966, straight from a kerosene fridge, now stands deserted and windowless, with the wind howling through. It used to take the best part of a week to go from Dibba to Khor Fakkan, by donkey. There were no roads or tracks and the villages had to be visited. We also used camels on certain patrols on the edge of the deep sands, mostly for practice. In those days the desert was clean and quiet, where one quickly came to terms with oneself.

It is good to remember the occasional much needed breaks, from the constant battering that the body took in an open Land Rover. Sitting with the soldiers, in a light breeze, with their cackle as they settled down to make coffee, the roasting of the green beans, the thump of the pestle in the mortar, the aroma of Arabic coffee with cardamom, unsweetened, was heavenly.

Today, the desert is not so clean, but strewn with litter, ranging from chip packets to beer cans and the only cackle is from expatriates charging around in 4WD vehicles that they do not, in most cases, know how to use. It is all a shame really, but I suppose it is the disease of the 20th/21st century and people don't care. In the cities, however, there is a much bigger effort to clean everything up and there are many new parks and gardens. The Municipalities have been magnificent in their planting schemes alongside the roads and on the roundabouts. Now there are quite a few vegetable farms, growing vegetables, salad and other crops. In 1966, there was one experimental farm at Digdagga, from which we received the odd box of lettuce, and most of the food was imported.

In 1966, few people in Europe knew where the Trucial States were on the map.

Now, very few people would not know where the UAE is situated. I feel I can look back with a certain amount of pride at the way it has all turned out. All of us played some little part in the difficult birth of this nation and hopefully we gave it a strong foundation to survive in the 21st century.

Appendix E

The Formation of the Trucial Oman Scouts

Kings Regulation no. 1 of 1951 established the Trucial Oman Levies under Article 82 of the Trucial States Order in Council of 1950. On 22 April 1950 a directive was issued clearly defining the role of the Levies by Sir Rupert Hay – HM Political Resident, Persian Gulf, and Mr. Ernest Bevin – UK Foreign Secretary. The directives were:

1. There shall be established and maintained in the Trucial States a Levy Force which shall be under the control and direction of the Political Resident in the Persian Gulf (under Foreign Office control). The Force shall be known as the Trucial Oman Levies.

The main duties of the Trucial Oman Levies are:-

a. To maintain peace and goodwill in the Trucial States.

b. To prevent or suppress any traffic in slaves.

c. To provide an escort for any British political representatives travelling in the Trucial States.

2. The Levies will only undertake operations at the express request of the Political Officer Trucial Coast (except in cases of emergency) or any person acting on his behalf. The Political Officer will outline the object of each operation and the Commander T.O.L. will decide how to deal with it.

3. The areas of the Trucial Coast Sheikhdoms will be clearly defined by directives issued by the Political Resident in Bahrain. The T.O.L. will not operate in any other areas.

4. The T.O.L. will not operate in a capital town or within the confines of the Ruler without express permission from the Political Officer or his representative.

5. Any person arrested by a member of the T.O.L., under his powers under King's Regulations, will be brought before the political representative as quickly as possible.

6. Steps must be taken to avoid giving offence to the Saudi Arabian authorities by any inconsiderate treatment of their nationals. Tribal movement should be reported and any attempts by Saudi officials to exercise control over Trucial Coast Sheikhdoms should be treated as trespass.

7. In any attack on the RAF Camp at Sharjah or any action being of mutiny or other emergency in the area, the Commander will place himself and the Levies under the orders of O.C. RAF.

8. No member of the Levies will in any fashion be allowed to undertake any political activity.

9. Budgetary expenditure of the Levies will be governed by the provisions of the Financial Regulations.

183

Initially the T.O.L. (Feb. 1951) were under the command of Major Hankin-Turvin, formerly of the Palestine Police and Arab Legion. It consisted of a cadre of 33 former Arab Legion soldiers and 60 locally recruited tribesmen. By April 1951 the Levies had started to move around the coastal area. They were billeted in RAF Sharjah near the old fort and only the very basics of accommodation had been provided against a very small budget. In 1955 the name of the Trucial Oman Levies was changed to the Trucial Oman Scouts.

Appendix F

The Foundation of the Emirates

In January 1968, Britain announced plans to leave the Gulf by the end of 1971. The Rulers of the Trucial States, led by Sheikh Zayed of Abu Dhabi and Sheikh Rashid of Dubai, along with the Rulers of Qatar and Bahrain met in February 1968 and agreed to try to form a federation. Three and a half years of discussions ensued on the structure of the new state, much complicated by the enormous differences between them.

As a result the Political Resident in the Gulf spent much time visiting each Ruler to coax them to reach agreement. It became increasingly clear that Bahrain and Qatar would opt to go on their own. In July 1971 a meeting of the Trucial States Council was held in Dubai – when all members were invited to lunch by the Trucial Oman Scouts. This was a very difficult day – but by the end of it six out of seven Sheikhdoms had signed to form the Union. The Sheikh of Ras al Khaimah declined to sign on the grounds that he refused "to be treated as a second class citizen and all men are equal before God", this being reference to the powers of veto granted to the two largest Sheikhdoms – Abu Dhabi and Dubai. Ras al Khaimah stood its ground based on the hope of oil discovery and on funds from Saudi Arabia to finance its own army. They later joined the Union in February 1972.

On 29 November 1971 the largest batch of T.O.S. recruits passed out from Manama and was posted to their various squadrons. This passing out parade was in effect the end of the Trucial Oman Scouts and the birth of the Union Defence Force. The period following was taken up with the last discussions on the forming of the Union itself. On 2nd December 1971, the formal Act of Union took place at the Palace of Sheikh Rashid of Dubai at Jumeirah – all Rulers attended except Ras al Khaimah.

Appendix G

The Defence Forces

The Trucial Oman Scouts was funded by the British Foreign Office and although it was in charge of defence of the whole area of the Trucial States, there was nonetheless a move by the various Sheikhs to set up their own private armies. As a result of anxiety at various key points such as Das Island (1965), Sheikh Shakhbut, the Ruler of Abu Dhabi, was the first to decide that he needed his own private army. Both the Political Resident and the Political Agent Abu Dhabi tried hard to dissuade him from this move, but he insisted. In 1965 the Abu Dhabi Defence Force was established with two British officers and a hundred men from the Trucial Oman Scouts.

This quite naturally started off a chain reaction amongst the other Sheikhdoms who at that time depended on the local recruited Police forces and the TOS. Quite soon afterward Sheikh Rashid of Dubai established the Dubai Defence Force with Ras al Khaimah and Sharjah following some five years later. The rush of recruitment into ADDF, with their higher rates of pay and better promotion chances, resulted in ADDF being stronger than TOS by 1971, the year of the Union.

The Sheikhs had become quite clearly worried, particularly after the British Prime Minister Harold Wilson's 1968 proclamation that all British troops were to be withdrawn from East of Suez by 1971. They therefore asked for a senior British military officer to be appointed to advise what steps should be taken with regard to defence. General Sir John Willoughby was appointed with a multi-force team in January 1969. They travelled throughout the Gulf, interviewing the various Rulers, with the result that a reasonable balance was put together that was acceptable.

It was evident that in this transitional period a vacuum was beginning to form within the defence force arena. This needed to be controlled until the new Union Defence Force could be in place. A Military Liaison Office (entitled the MOD) was established therefore in 1971 under the command of a previous TOS Commander, with the aim of providing a controlled link between the Political Resident and his agents and the Trucial States Rulers. The months slipped by and there was still no decision on the future of the Scouts. Proposals were in fact being put together, which resulted in basic acceptance by all Rulers. This meant that the Trucial Oman Scouts were to become part of a new force of about brigade strength called the Union Defence Force.

The transition from TOS to UDF took place at Manama on 29 November 1971, when a large batch of recruits passed out from basic training.

Further Reading

The British Army Review, Number 17, October 1963

Arabian Adventure by Anthony Shepherd, Collins 1961

The Trucial Oman Scouts, The Story of a Bedouin Force by Michael Mann, Michael Russell 1994

Two Alpha Lima by Peter Clayton, Janus Publishing Co., 1994

Now the Dust has Settled, Memories of War and Peace, 1939 – 1994, Freddie de Butts, Tabb House, 1995

The Emirates, Witness to a Metamorphosis, Donald Hawley, Michael Russell (Publishing) Ltd, 2007

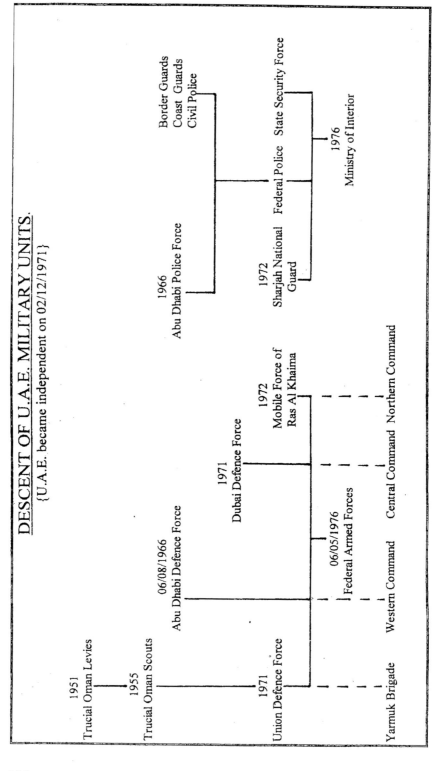

DESCENT OF U.A.E. MILITARY UNITS.
{U.A.E. became independent on 02/12/1971}

1951
Trucial Oman Levies

1955
Trucial Oman Scouts

06/08/1966
Abu Dhabi Defence Force

1971
Dubai Defence Force

1972
Mobile Force of Ras Al Khaima

1971
Union Defence Force

06/05/1976
Federal Armed Forces

Yarmuk Brigade   Western Command   Central Command   Northern Command

1966
Abu Dhabi Police Force

Border Guards
Coast Guards
Civil Police

1972
Sharjah National Guard   Federal Police   State Security Force

1976
Ministry of Interior

Reproduced with kind permission of the Orders & Medals Research Society, from their article on the TOS by O. Wain

Index

Abdulaziz bin M Al Qassimi 171
Abdullah bin Ali al Ka'abi 145,
152, 178
Abdullah bin Salim al Ka'abi 45,
47, 169
Abdullah Gadaya, Sergeant 110,
174
Ahmad bin Rashid, Sheikh,
Ruler of Umm al Quwain 169
Ahmed Ali, Sgt. 126
Adam Sheikh Na'im 118
Adami, Major C.J. 170
Addison, Lt.Col A.E.G. 169/170
Ali Khalifa, Signals Corporal 163
Allfree, Maj. P.S. 169
Anderson, Brig. D.W. 169/170
Anstee, Maj. D.G.M. 122, 126,
135, 171, 179
Arab Legion 20, 21
Arabsat 83, 85, 87
Armitage, Capt. K. 170
Arthur, Sir Geoffrey,
Ambassador Kuwait, Political
Resident Persian Gulf 72, 92
Ash, Capt. Tim 114
Atiq bin Murad al Abdulla, SSM
110, 130, 137, 160, 163, 168,
174, 178
BAC, British Aircraft Corporation
51, 80-83, 86, 89, 90
Baddeley, Capt. M.St.C. 169/170
BAe, British Aerospace 86-91
Balfour Paul, Glen 122, 126
Bannister, Capt. D.J.C. 169/170
Barnett, Lt.Col. Graham 179
Barron, Maj. L.N. 159, 160, 171,
178, 179
Bartholomew, Col. H.J. 65,
169/170
Baugniet, Col. M.L.A. 169/170
Baxter, Maj. P.M. 169/170
Beckhurst, Maj. V.W. 169/170
Bedford, Maj. R.T. 115, 170
Bidgood, Lt.Col. J.P.S. 169/170
Birley, Major, MFH 13
Bishr bin Bidr 130, 152
Boota Khan 10, 11
Boots Company 112, 166, 175
Boustead, Col. Sir Hugh 133
Bowen, Col. T.J. 45, 169/170
Bowman, Eric 75
Briggs, Jack 114, 182
Bromley, Sqn.Ldr. Harry 128, 134
Brown, Major Bob 148
Brown, John 71, 72

Buckmaster, Martin (later
Viscount) 112, 146, 157
Budd, Maj. Tim 23-5, 113, 126,
136, 138, 153, 156, 169/170,
179
Bullard, Maj. W.A. 169/170
Bullocke, Brig. C.W.G. 169/170
Burnand, Capt. P.V. 169/170
Burns, Maj. B.S. 170, 171
Burnett, Maj. R.F.W. 169/170
Cambridge University 20, 23
Carson, Maj. E. 169/170
Carter, Col. S.L.A. 24, 34, 51, 57,
62, 65, 169/170
Cawston, Caroline 20
Cawston, Celia 86
Cawston, Mary 20, 78
Cawston, Peter 86
Cawston, Lt.Col. S.A.R. 38, 92-3,
167, 169/170
Chambers, Captain Peter 168
Chandler, Sir Colin, Chairman
BAe Aircraft Group 90-1
Charrington, Maj. G.A. 38,
169/170
Chubb, Maj. P.F. 52, 169/170
Cochrane-Dyet, Maj. R.S. 126,
171, 179
Cocking, Brig. N.H. 169/170
Cornish, Maj. G.S.C. 114, 170,
179
Cosgrove, Maj. D.J 113, 117,
169/170, 178, 179
Cousens, Maj. J. 133-5, 143, 171
Courtney, Sergeant 155
Craig-Adams, Maj. I.M. 45,
169/170
Criddle, Capt. C.W. 169/170
Cross Kelly, Maj. Dick 100
Crotale 81-2
Crouch, Capt. I.J. 114, 170
Curtis, Capt. J.M. 3,92-3, 126,
163, 171
D'Abo, Philip 180
Deane Drummond,
Lt.Col.Anthony, Comd. 22 SAS
26-7, 29-31
de Beaujeu, Col. D.L. 169/170
de Butts, Col. F.M. 103-4, 106,
113, 122, 126, 136, 168, 170,
179
Deolali School of Artillery 5
Devereux, Capt. J.A.N. 171
de Vivenot, Maj. F.X. 169/170
Dinnin, Maj. R.H.H. 141-2,

147-152, 171, 179
Dunbar, Brig. Charles 152, 160
Dykins, Capt. D. 171, 179
Eid, David 115, 181
Faisal bin Sultan al Qassimi,
Capt./Sheikh 51, 167, 171
Feltham, Lt.Col. R.H.B. 106, 113,
144, 155, 161, 165, 170, 177,
179
Feltham, Liz 106, 117, 144, 161,
177
Ffrench-Blake, Capt. A. 171
Fisher, Capt. J.O. 169/170
Fitzgerald, Capt. M. 171
Foster, Bob 109
Foulds, Capt. D.E. 169/170
Gauvain, Capt. A.de P. 171
Ghalib bin Ali, Imam of Oman
23, 35
Gibson, Maj. Tom 103
Glazebrook, Maj. D. 113, 170,
179
Glubb, Sir John, Lt.Gen., Comd.
Jordan Arab Legion 20-1
Goodchild, Capt. D. 159, 171,
178-9
Gouriet, Maj. J.P 169/170
Gowlett, Capt. G. 171
Graham, John 72
Gray Mackenzie Co. 121, 124
Green, Lt.Col. R.G.M. 169/170
Gregory, Maj. J.F.H. 169/170
Greig, Ian, Captain R.A. 5, 8
Halford, Lt.Col. J.B.J. 169/170
Hallidie, Maj. N.A. 169/170
Halstead, Maj. J.D. 105, 108-9,
114, 116, 122-4, 126-8, 130,
133, 135-7, 139, 141, 143, 146-
7, 151-2, 171-3, 176-7
Hall, Sir Arnold, Chairman of
Hawker Siddeley 89
Hammick, Maj. C.C. 169/170
Harford, Maj. G.A. 169/170
Hargrove, Maj. S.J.A. 169/170
Harris. Capt. N.D.J. 149, 171, 173,
175, 179
Hassan Said, Lt. 110, 123, 126,
128, 130, 135, 137, 151-3, 156,
171-2, 178
Hastie, David 87
Hawker Siddeley 83-6, 89, 90
Hawley, Sir Donald, Political
Agent 49, 50, 92
Henchman, D. 171
Hickman, Peter 84

Hillyard, Lt.Col. E.H. 169/170
Holyer, Brig., Comd. L.F.P.G. 122
Hussein, HM King of Jordan 21, 88, 143
Issa bin Sulman, Sheikh, Ruler of Bahrein 124
Ive, Col. K.C.P. 139,146-7, 159, 161, 163, 165, 168, 170
Ive, Jeanette 139, 165
Jackson, Sergeant 155, 161
Jebel Akhdar 23, 26, 27, 29, 31, 35, 48, 54
Jinnah, Mohammed Ali 13, 14
Jones, Maj. E.R.L. 169/170
Kennedy, Pat 129, 177
Khuda Baksh, Subedar 7
King, Maj. A.H.B. 169/170
Kumaramangalam, Lt. Col. PP, 'Colonel K' 13, 14
Laing, Maj. A.H.169/170
Lamb, Archie, Political Agent 122, 126
Landau, Lt.Col. J.S. 169/170
Langdale, Maj. J.K. 170, 179
Little, Maj. Mike 143
Lee, Maj. B.S. 169/170
Lomas Michael 137
Lovett, Capt. Hugh 155
Luce, Sir William 111, 126
Lumby, Maj. C.W.T. 169/170
Lygo, Admiral Sir Raymond, Chairman BAe Dynamics Group 81
Mason, Maj. A.C. 169/170
McClellan, Capt. M. 171
McKinnon, Brig. A.W.M. 169/170
MECAS, Middle East Centre for Arab Studies 20-22, 175
MEDEA, Middle East Direct Export Assistance 167
Merrylees, Lt.Col. D.L. 169/170
Middlemiss, Maj. Peter, HQ SAF Muscat 26
Mohammed Ali, driver 149
Mohammed Iqbal 105
Mohd. Saleh, Maj. 171
Morris, Maj. J.D. 114, 163, 170
Mountbatten, Viscount, Viceroy of India 14
Mul.(Lt.) Midfa 170
Muhammad bin Hamad, Sheikh, Ruler of Fujairah 41, 169
Nagib Ali, Staff Sergeant 149
Neild, Capt. D.E.G. 117, 122, 126, 135, 147-8, 153, 159, 169/170, 171-2, 179-80
Nuttall, Simon, Deputy Political Agent 122, 126
Obeid Ali, Lt. 124, 126

Owens, Richard 124
Oxford University 23, 25
Parkin, Maj. A.R. 170, 179
Parsons, Lt.Col. M.D. 169, 170
Pattinson, Capt. John 80
Peat, Maj. J.W.B 169/170
Perkins, Maj.Gen. Ken 79
Pitman, Capt. R.C. 171
Pitt, Capt. J.K. 113, 117, 139, 141, 147, 160, 164, 170, 179
Potier, Capt. J.R. 170
Pott, Maj. R.J.L 41, 50, 51, 169/170
Prescott, P. 171
Pyle, Maj. R.L. 169/170
Qaboos, HM Sultan of Oman 173-4
Rapier 51, 80-3, 86-9
Rashid bin Humaid, Sheikh, Ruler of Ajman 52-4, 169
Rashid bin Subayha 152
Rashid bin Said al Makhtoum, Sheikh, Ruler of Dubai 114, 122, 126, 169, 184
Ricketts, Maj. A.P.P. 171, 179
Roberts, David, Political Agent Dubai 112, 115, 150, 161
Roberts, Goronwy 72
Roden, Capt. H. 169/170
Royal Hampshire Regiment 97, 155, 165, 175-6
Rundell, Lt.Col. A.J. 169/170
Said Alam Khan Afridi 106, 135-6
Sa'id bin Taimur, Sultan of Oman 23, 31, 35, 45, 54, 169
Salem bin Mohammed al Qassimi, Sheikh 167
Salim bin Mussalim al Said, 2/Lt. 117, 124, 126-7, 130, 135, 137, 152, 171-4
Saqr bin Muhammad, Sheikh, Ruler of Ras al Khaimah 41, 169
Saqr bin Sultan al Qassimi, Sheikh, Ruler of Sharjah 57, 169
Savage, Maj. J.G. 169/170
Seaton-Brown, Carl 156
Severn, Maj. D.B. 126, 171
Sewell, Maj. R.J. 169/170
Shakhbut bin Sultan, Ruler of Abu Dhabi 25, 39, 93, 117, 119, 121, 124, 126, 169, 184
Shepherd, David 130
Shepherd, Maj.G.A. 169/170
Shields, Lt. R. 152, 158, 171
Shotter, Maj. R.L. 113, 170, 179
Sibbick, Lt. R. 169/170
Smiley, Col. David, Comd. Sultan

Armed Forces, Muscat 26
Smith, Maj. B.R.C. 169/170
Smith, Bernard 101-2
Special Air Service, 22 SAS Regt. 22, 27-31, 34-5, 37
Spinneys 115-6, 121, 124, 167, 176, 180 1
Squires, Capt. C.J. 114, 170
Stevens, Maj. W.H. 169/170
Stockdale, Maj. W.F. (Jim) 41, 155, 157, 169/170, 171
Stockwell, Capt. Miles 172
Suleiman bin Himyar, Sheikh of the Bani Riyam 54
Swindells, Capt. S.W. 114, 170, 179
Swinhoe, Maj. P. 114, 128, 170
Talib bin Ali, bro. of Ghalib bin Ali 35
Taylor, Capt. E.B. 171, 174
Taylor, Col. O.B. 101, 169/170
Theobalds, Capt. S. 170
Tibby, Maj. Don 115, 170, 182
Timbrell, Col. Kenneth, OC British Troops Sharjah 138, 164
Timmis, Maj. M.F. 169/170
Tinker, Brig.Ted, CLFPG 23, 26
Tullet, Graham 100
Vining, Lt.Col. M.E. 169/170
Vivian, Graham, Oman Gendarmerie 137
Wallace, Maj. R.C. 114, 170, 179
Wallerstein, Lt.Col. A.B. 169/170
Weir, Maj. R.L.G.169/170
Whitelaw, Capt. R.J.G. 105, 113, 116, 162-3, 165, 170, 178-80
Wilkes, Capt. L. 171
Williams, Capt. D.G. 170
Williams, Maj. H.R. 170
Willoughby, Lt. Gen. Sir John 104
Wilson, Maj. E.B. (Tug) 123-4, 126, 132
Wilson, Maj. K. 45, 49, 122, 126, 159, 169/170, 171
Wilson, Lt.Col. Sandy 165
Wilson, Sergeant 116
Wontner, Capt. Charles 123
Woodburn, Brig. C.W. 169/170
Woodruffe, Capt. D.N.S. 169/170
Wootten, Bertie, Air Commodore (retd.) 83
Wright, Lt.Col. Robin 72
Young, Capt. A. 116, 171
Zaid bin Shaker, Sharif, Comd. Jordan Armed Forces 88-9
Zayed bin Sultan, Sheikh, Ruler of Abu Dhabi 25-6, 45, 93, 121, 123-6, 129-30 ,133, 138-9, 141, 143,146, 169, 184